HAUNTED BOSTON HARBOR

HAUNTED BOSTON HARBOR

SAM BALTRUSIS

Haunted America

Published by Haunted America
A Division of The History Press
Charleston, SC
www.historypress.net

Front cover: Photographer Frank C. Grace's photo of the historic Boston Light on Little Brewster captures the eerie, something-wicked-this-way-comes vibe of the iconic, three-centuries-old lighthouse in Boston Harbor.

First published 2016

ISBN 978-1-5316-9926-0

Library of Congress Control Number: 2016936013

CONTENTS

Acknowledgements

After writing *Haunted Boston Harbor*, my internal batteries are recharged and I'm grateful to have spent months exploring the mysteries of Boston Harbor as a tour guide with Boston Harbor Cruises. Thanks go to my spirit squad from the historical-based ghost tour Boston Haunts, including Nick Cox and Hank Fay, for helping me rouse the dead and give a voice to those long departed. The Haunted Boston Harbor boat tour I produced in 2014 on the Massachusetts Bay Lines' *Samuel Clemens* helped shape the tone and lore featured in the book. Major thanks to the handful of paranormal investigators and researchers who helped make *Haunted Boston Harbor* a reality, including lighthouse expert Jeremy D'Entremont, Rachel Hoffman, Tina Storer and James DePaul from Paranormal Xpeditions; authors Cindy Vallar, Joni Mayhan, MaryLee Trettenero and Peter Muise; Joe "Jiggy" Webb from the weekly podcast *Paranormal Hood*; and Jeffrey Doucette, a veteran tour guide who appeared in my first book, *Ghosts of Boston: Haunts of the Hub*. I would like to give my friend and copy editor Andrew Warburton a supernatural slap on the back. He helped me uncover some of the skeletal secrets featured in this monstrous project. Thanks to my mother, Deborah Hughes Dutcher, for being there when I need her most and my friends for their continued support. I would also like to thank Karmen Cook from The History Press for her help during the process of putting this book together. Special thanks go to folklorist and author Edward Rowe Snow. His passion for Boston Harbor lives on and is felt by the thousands who bravely creep through Fort Warren's dark hallway on Georges Island during the summer.

INTRODUCTION

The Lady in Black summoned me here. However, as I searched every nook and cranny of Georges Island during a five-month gig as a historical narrator in Boston Harbor, the ghost of Melanie Lanier—as the Lady in Black is otherwise called—refused to reveal herself. She was playing hard to get.

"Something touched me in there, and it wasn't human!" screamed a girl running out of the corridor of dungeons after a field trip to Fort Warren at Georges Island. "It was the Lady in Black," she said convincingly.

The girl looked mortified.

This was just one of the strange events that occurred during the summer of 2014 when I gave historical tours with Boston Harbor Cruises and traveled on large vessels carrying passengers back and forth to various islands in the outer harbor. I spent most afternoons during the summer searching for a repeat experience of a shadow figure that I'd seen there seven years before. No such luck.

I frequently heard screams emanating from Fort Warren's haunted ramparts. However, it was usually one of the kids touring the dark hallway in the southeast battery.

The location that Edward Rowe Snow said was the Lady in Black's haunt was in the front of the fort. It's still accessible, but it's extremely dusty and dark.

In 2007, I moved back to Boston from Florida and had a ghostly experience while touring the ramparts of Fort Warren at Georges Island. Out of the corner of my eye, I noticed an all-black shadow figure. I looked again, and

Fort Warren, built from 1833 to 1861, served as a prison for captured Confederate soldiers during the Civil War. The spiral staircase leads to the bowels of the fort on Georges Island, which is home of the Lady in Black legend. *Photo by Sam Baltrusis.*

it was gone. At this point, I had never heard the Lady in Black legend. I just intuitively knew Georges Island had some sort of psychic residue. While researching Fort Warren's history, my interest in Boston's haunted past gradually became a passion. History repeats itself, and it was my job to

Discovered by John Smith in 1614, Boston Harbor is the most historic and arguably the most haunted port in America. This archival photo from 1906 captures the changing landscape of the waterfront, which was backfilled to accommodate the city's growing need for land. *Photo by Detroit Publishing Company.*

uncover the truth and give a voice to those without a voice—even though most of the stories turned out to be tales from the crypt.

Lawrence, a fellow Boston Harbor Cruises tour guide and former park ranger, insisted that ghosts do not inhabit Georges Island, adding that the Lady in Black legend was completely made up by folklorist Edward Rowe Snow.

"I spent so many nights there, I would know," he said, as we passed Nix's Mate en route to the mainland. "However, I would say the island has a spirit. Some rangers say the island's energy, or spirit, welcomes people."

In hindsight, I've decided that my encounter on Georges in 2007 was the island's spirit welcoming me. However, ghosts can almost certainly be found nearby.

While several of the thirty-four islands have paranormal activity, Boston Harbor's Little Brewster is allegedly the most haunted. The mysterious Boston Light, one of the five remaining Coast Guard–manned lighthouses in America, stands eerily on the rocky, two-acre island. It's located behind Georges Island and can be spotted from the ramparts, which I explored regularly during the summer of 2014. While I was giving historical tours, the lighthouse was closed for much-needed repairs in preparation for its three-hundred-year anniversary.

Boston Light reopened in 2015 and has once again become a Boston Harbor hot spot.

Photographer Frank C. Grace, his father and I took a ferry out to Little Brewster. It was a rainy, overcast day—perfect weather for a ghostly encounter.

Coincidentally, we visited hours before Boston Light's 299-year anniversary on September 14, 2015, and the island was buzzing with excitement from both the living and the dead. The volunteers at the historic lighthouse were quick to confirm that Little Brewster was indeed haunted.

"You hear ghost stories all the time," remarked Val, a veteran tour guide. "One day, I had climbed all the way to the top and I heard phantom footsteps behind me and there was definitely no one else in the lighthouse."

Other volunteers have mentioned hearing what sound like congo drums, possibly Native American tribal rhythms, on the island, without a plausible explanation.

Jeremy D'Entremont, historian for the American Lighthouse Foundation and author of *The Lighthouse Handbook New England*, confirmed the ghostly legends associated with Boston Light. "Coast Guard keepers experienced odd things and generally blamed it on 'George,' meaning George Worthylake, the first keeper, who drowned in 1718," he told me. "The Coast Guard Auxiliary Watchstanders who spend shifts there today have also seen strange things."

On the way back, we passed by many of the islands I fell in love with during the summer of 2014. Nix's Mate, the smallest of the harbor islands, seemed particularly ominous. Marked by a black-and-white beacon and completely submerged during high tide, the freakishly small island is where pirates were kept in a crude contraption known as a gibbet cage, an invention of the Puritans. They would showcase the pirates as sort of a cautionary tale. While narrating Boston Harbor tours, I was pushed from my seat by an unseen force multiple times when passing this spot. It was so intense that I physically tied myself to my chair. One time, I was pushed so hard that I almost fell off the top deck of the vessel.

Disgruntled ghost pirates? Yep, Boston Harbor has them.

Of course, I had multiple encounters while researching the various haunts featured in *Haunted Boston Harbor*. The most profound was during an exploration of the USS *Constitution*, or Old Ironsides. The famous vessel was scheduled to be dry-docked for a three-year hiatus. I had seen it multiple times in all its majestic glory in Boston Harbor. It was breathtaking to watch the three-masted frigate sail past my vessel; it brought me to tears.

According to naval officer Wesley Bishop, *Ghost Hunters* was scheduled to investigate the oldest commissioned naval vessel still afloat. And yes, the uniformed crew did strongly believe that Old Ironsides was, in fact, haunted. "No enemy died on board, so if there are ghosts, they're my fellow crew members who died long ago from battle-related wounds or the elements,"

Comprising thirty-four islands and spanning fifty square miles, Boston Harbor is a geological anomaly because it's the only drumlin swarm in the United States that intersects a coastline. *Courtesy of the Boston Public Library, Print Department.*

Bishop told me. "I haven't had an encounter, but several of my [living] crew members have."

Meanwhile, his fellow naval officer friend chimed in, "There are definitely ghosts on board."

While I was peeking into the berthing area known as "the rack," I swore I saw a shadow figure dart by me. Of course, multiple reports have been made of a sailor wearing a navy blue jacket and gold buttons. Ellen MacNeil, who has investigated the USS *Constitution* with her team, SPIRITS of New England, confirmed that the vessel is paranormally active.

"Is it haunted? Oh, hell yes," MacNeil told *Haunted Boston Harbor*. Her team investigated the *Constitution* in 2010 over a two-day period. "We totally freaked out the captain with our audio and video evidence. With 308 deaths on the ship, mainly from illness not battle, the ship is very much loved and protected by these lost souls who were playful, curious and responsive to us being there."

In addition to the USS *Constitution*, I had an up-close-and-personal encounter with the extremely haunted *Charles W. Morgan*. One sunny afternoon, the last wooden whaleship in the world cruised past my vessel in the harbor. The *Morgan* is supposedly haunted by a nineteenth-century sailor smoking a pipe. It was so surreal to experience this ancient vessel sail by me.

I also had a few bizarre experiences on the mainland. One sunny June afternoon, I was walking up State Street near the Old State House. A

Electronic voice phenomena of a male voice have been captured near Fort Warren's guardhouse area. Alexander Hamilton Stephens, the vice president of the Confederacy, was confined in the makeshift prison on Georges Island in 1865. *Photo by Sam Baltrusis.*

Clydesdale-type horse—his name is Prince—was carrying two passengers to the heart of Boston's Revolutionary War past. The carriage driver named Becky, a saucy brunette, was stunned when the horse stopped mid-trot, raised his hoof as if he was spooked by an unseen force and looked in my direction. "Whoa, it must be a ghost," Becky said without hesitation. "It's the ghosts of the revolution."

Apparently, horses are sensitives, too. If Becky only knew.

While giving tours during the summer of 2014, a co-worker at Boston Harbor Cruises captured an electronic voice phenomenon while exploring Georges Island one afternoon. He spent the day with his brother exploring the fort and captured a voice of what sounded like a man. "You can hear breathing, and then it says something," he told me, playing the recording over and over.

"It sounds like it says 'get out' or something similar," I told him.

What's even more fascinating is that the male voice saying, "Get out" in his impromptu EVP sounded southern. Could it be a Confederate soldier?

One year later, I ventured out to Fort Warren and crawled through the original corridor of dungeons. I found the coffin used by Edward Rowe Snow to retell the Lady in Black legend. It was covered in dust and cobwebs.

A message from the vice president of the Confederacy, Alexander Hamilton Stephens, popped into my head. His quote: "All the genius I have lies in this."

I laughed. It all made sense now. There is no Lady in Black. The ghost is a Confederate soldier or possibly even the cranky spirit of Stephens. I shivered in the beauty and the madness of the moment.

I crawled out of Fort Warren's corridor of dungeons armed with my latest tale from the crypt. Melanie Lanier is totally made up. The Lady in Black is a man.

Chapter 1

Asylum Haunts

Boston Harbor was a literal dumping ground for the city's undesirables and those traditionally marginalized by the status quo. Asylums, or institutions built for the poor, orphaned, sick and mentally ill were commonplace on a handful of the islands throughout the harbor.

"For centuries, Bostonians used the harbor islands to sequester and provide for those suffering from physical and social ills," reported the *Boston Phoenix*. "Locals have grown up believing that many of these sites are haunted. They are: if not by ghosts, then by the twisted and shameful legacy of what happened in these places."

Based on the intense residual energy at many of the former asylums scattered throughout Boston Harbor, it would make sense that many of the people who lived in these buildings left behind a psychic imprint of sorts, especially if neglect or trauma was involved.

One hypothesis, developed in the 1970s and known as the Stone Tape theory, speculates that an environment can absorb energy from a high-tension event, such as an untimely death or a suicide. The theory is a possible explanation for the alleged paranormal activity reported on the islands of Boston Harbor, including lights flickering and inexplicable screams. A residual haunting is like a videotaped event that plays over and over. Residual spirits are not intelligent entities and can't interact with the living. However, it's possible that a few lost souls still linger on the islands where they were formerly sequestered.

Rachel Hoffman, investigator with the all-female team called Paranormal Xpeditions, said it's possible that an aura of disaster has psychically imprinted

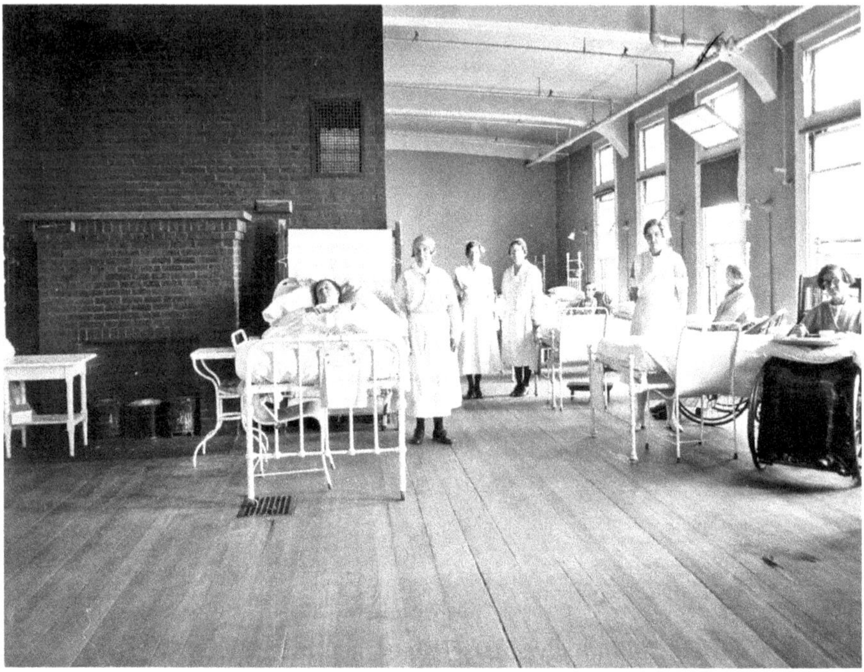

Long Island's Chronic Disease Hospital and almshouse was home to 1,400 patients and inmates in the 1940s and was staffed by hundreds of nurses, doctors and employees. *Courtesy of the Boston Public Library, Print Department.*

itself on the islands, especially those that formerly housed tuberculosis clinics, poorhouses or mental institutions. "We believe that asylums are higher in paranormal activity due to the amount of personal anguish suffered by the ill and also the nurses who were understaffed," explained Hoffman. "We oftentimes hear them going about their daily activities as if they don't know they are dead."

Hoffman appeared on Zak Bagan's *Paranormal Challenge*, during which her team investigated the extremely haunted Rolling Hills Asylum in East Bethany, New York. On the Travel Channel show, Paranormal Xpeditions captured a "class A" EVP of a female voice saying, "Don't touch me again" followed by the sound of a straightjacket slapping down after a blood-curdling shriek.

"We believe it was a confrontation between a nurse and a patient," said Hoffman. "I believe it was residual activity and probably repeats itself consistently because the patient is unaware that she has died."

The veteran paranormal investigator believes that the ghosts haunting old asylums are both intelligent and residual. "We have come across spirits

Long Island, marked by a red-and-white water tank, inspired the fictional Ashecliffe Hospital for the Criminally Insane in author Dennis Lehane's book *Shutter Island*. *Photo by Jason Baker.*

that are nasty in nature and tend to carry on being aggressive even after death," Hoffman said. "We also run into child spirits, which are the ones to us that tend to be intelligent and receptive. We generally bring candy or toys as trigger objects to evoke a response. Kids love candy and shiny toys and usually approach us easily, as we have a mothering nature to our crew of all females."

The asylums in Boston Harbor deviate a bit from the so-called insane asylums we've seen portrayed in pop culture, specifically on TV shows like *American Horror Story: Asylum* and movies like Martin Scorsese's *Shutter Island*. However, they did exist in other areas like Danvers, Medfield and Taunton.

Cambridge's "Jolly" Jane Toppan is an extreme example of a human monster who formerly worked and eventually died in one of those inhumane institutions. Born in 1854, Toppan began training to be a nurse at Cambridge Hospital in 1885. There she would overdose her patients with morphine and change their medical charts to hide evidence of their intake. She was known as "Jolly" Jane because of her sugary-sweet demeanor. However, Toppan got her jollies by killing her victims and jumping into bed with them after she poisoned them. She would wrap her limbs around her dying patients and get sexual gratification from feeling the life leaving their frail bodies. She left a trail of bodies at Cambridge Hospital and was moved to Boston's Mass General in 1890.

After years of murdering innocent patients, she was implicated in 1902 and was sent to the Taunton Insane Hospital, where she died in 1938. There she refused to eat because she was afraid staffers at the insane asylum had poisoned her food. From a paranormal perspective, it would make sense that the female serial killer's spirit lingers at the spot where she died.

When it comes to asylums in Massachusetts, including the handful of institutions in Boston Harbor, fact is definitely stranger than fiction.

"It's tough to invent anything more messed up than what actually happened at Massachusetts's network of public mental hospitals," wrote Scott Kearnan in the *Boston Phoenix*. "Our state's institutional memories are riddled with sordid tales of deplorable physical conditions, sexual misconduct and cruelly unusual torture masquerading as treatment."

DEER ISLAND

Don't let the dinosaur egg–shaped sludge digesters from the sewage treatment facility fool you. Deer Island is marred by tragedy and stained with the blood of hundreds of innocents who were confined in one of the most horrific untold genocides in American history.

For the Native Americans quarantined on the 185-acre dumping ground, Deer Island was known as Devil's Island.

A group of native people were converted to Christianity by the Reverend John Eliot. Known as the "praying Indians," they were captured one night in October 1675 and were quarantined on the barren island, their captors fueled by fear of the impending King Philip's War. Eliot, a British minister who had fled to Boston in 1631, had painstakingly translated the Bible into their native tribal language. Many of the innocent men, women and children were holding their Bibles when they were forced to fend for themselves on what was then a desolate island in Boston Harbor.

"Deer Island became a place of internment in the winter of 1675–76 for approximately 500 Native Americans, whom Europeans had removed from their homes and villages," reported the National Park Service's website. "Many of the imprisoned Native Americans died that winter without access to adequate food or shelter."

Millions of gallons of sewage are pumped through the dinosaur egg–shaped tanks known as sludge digestors. The Deer Island Sewage Treatment facility was ordered by a federal judge after the citizens of Boston filed a lawsuit to clean up the harbor. *Photo by Frank C. Grace.*

Contrary to the NPS report, there were up to 1,100 "praying Indians" kept on Deer Island, and historians believe that more could have lived there who went unrecorded. The Native Americans, demonized by the colonists, were dropping at an alarming rate. Many of them were on the shoreline praying for God to help. No one came.

The Reverend Eliot made several attempts to deliver food, but the angry townspeople stopped him by trying to capsize his vessel. A group of men planned to massacre the natives—or, as Malden's Abram Hill worded it, they intended to "destroy ye Indians." The rogue slayers never made it out to Deer Island. However, hundreds of natives died anyway from the elements and lack of food.

During the spring of 1676, a rescue vessel was sent to retrieve the few "praying Indians" who were still alive. The handful who did survive were rumored to have been sold as slaves.

Paranormal investigators believe this tragedy left an aura of disaster on Deer Island. People have reported inexplicable cries and a residual haunting of tribal drums on the island over the years. However, the screams of the Native Americans were just a precursor to the horrors yet to unfold on this cursed land.

When millions fled Ireland to seek refuge from the Great Famine in the mid-1800s, Deer Island became a quarantine facility for thousands of Irish immigrants. "In June 1847, the City of Boston established a hospital on Deer Island," confirmed the NPS website. "Approximately 4,800 men, women and children were admitted for treatment in the years from 1847 to 1849. Many recovered, but more than 800 died."

There's one notorious haunting in Boston tied to hundreds of Irish children whose lives ended abruptly on Deer Island. According to lore, a teen spirit with a soiled dress has been a regular visitor at the Central Burying Ground. She's believed to be one of the many children buried in a mass grave in the pauper cemetery on the corner of Tremont and Boylston Streets.

According to the late, great ghost expert Jim McCabe, the young female spirit is a teen girl "with long red hair, sunken cheekbones and a mud-splattered gray dress on." On a rainy afternoon in the 1970s, she paid a visit to a dentist named Dr. Matt Rutger, who reportedly experienced "a total deviation from reality as most of us know it." According to Holly Nadler's *Ghosts of Boston Town*, Rutger was checking out the gravestone carvings. He felt a tap on his shoulder and then a violent yank on his collar. No one was there.

As Rutger was bolting from the cemetery, he noticed something out of the corner of his eye. "I saw a young girl standing motionless in the rear corner of the cemetery, staring at me intently," he said. The mischievous spirit then reappeared near the graveyard's gate, almost fifty yards from the initial encounter. Then the unthinkable happened. "He somehow made it by her to Boylston Street, and even though he couldn't see her, he felt her hand slip inside his coat pocket, take out his keys and dangle them in midair before dropping them," McCabe recounted.

Others have spotted the teen spirit over the years. I've seen photos of a full-bodied apparition of what appears to be a girl wearing a bonnet. According to legend, Dr. Rutger was doing an etching at a mass grave for children who died from tuberculosis on Deer Island. Indeed, a cemetery on the island called Rest Haven is believed to be the final resting spot for the people who died there in the 1800s. However, ghost lore enthusiasts claim the ghost girl regularly encountered in Central Burying Ground is one of the thousands of Irish immigrants who fled to Boston to seek refuge.

In 1850, an almshouse, or asylum for the poor, was built on Deer Island to house the city's paupers. The structure became a short-term prison in 1896. The facility was a house of correction until 1991. According to *A Short History of Nearly Everything*, experiments were done on the prisoners. The

A quarantine hospital was built on Deer Island in 1847. Thousands of Irish immigrants were admitted to the asylum during the smallpox epidemic. Hundreds died and are buried in a mass grave on the island's northern hill. In 1850, an almshouse was built and became a prison in 1896. The facility was a house of correction until 1991. *Courtesy of the Boston Public Library, Print Department.*

facility generally held short-term offenders whose crimes ranged from public drunkenness to disorderly conduct.

According to people who spent time in the Deer Island House of Industry, cruel and unusual punishment was the norm. In fact, one woman reached out to me to help solve what is believed to be the unsolved murder of her great-great-grandfather. "His name was John Barry. He was murdered in April 1894 on Deer Island where he had been on and off for about fifteen years," wrote Julie H. via e-mail. "The *Boston Globe* articles I unearthed helped me confirm he is my ancestor. However, not long after the murder the 'case' went cold, and I assume the suspect was never captured. There is nothing about the murder other than the suspect's name on the date of the murder and the word *escaped*."

Escaped? No reports of a prison escape in 1894 have been found. Besides, based on the structure's design, an escape would have been nearly impossible. Based purely on intuition, it sounds like an inside job or coverup of sorts.

Deer Island Lighthouse, built in 1890, was the scene of tragedy in 1916, when assistant light keeper Joseph McCabe slipped on a rock and drowned in Boston Harbor. *Courtesy of the Boston Public Library, Print Department.*

The waterway, known as the Shirley Gut channel, that separates Deer Island from Winthrop was filled in after the 1938 New England nor'easter. So it's highly unlikely a prisoner could have escaped the facility and then swum in the harbor without getting caught.

In fact, there was an attempted escape in 1933, and all four men were apprehended.

As far as ghosts are concerned, there's a legend involving the Deer Island Lighthouse, which was built in 1890. "After the Coast Guard took over the light, officer-in-charge John Baxter played a trick on a new crewmember," reported LighthouseFriends.com. "Knowing the surf was rising and soon the light would be shaking, he said, 'I want to warn you. We have ghosts out here.' Soon the coffee cup on the table began to dance as if in proof."

Jeremy D'Entremont, historian for the American Lighthouse Foundation, confirmed the ghostly pranks at the Deer Island Lighthouse. "One of the early keepers at Deer Island Light drowned near the lighthouse," he said.

"Later, Coast Guard keepers would tell new arrivals that the place was haunted. One told me that he made a coffee cup slide across a table and convinced a new arrival that the ghost did it. Of course, the fact that the whole place was on a slight slant is what made the coffee cup slide."

As D'Entremont mentioned, one tragedy at the Deer Island Lighthouse could have resulted in an actual haunting. Joseph McCabe accepted the post as assistant light keeper in 1908. He found the isolation unbearable and had a piano delivered to the lighthouse to "break the monotony of the lonely life in the isolated tower," reported the *Boston Globe* in 1913. He met a woman, Gertrude Walter, in East Boston and left his post on February 16, 1916, to help his soon-to-be-wife address wedding invitations. On the trek back, he hopped on a rock and tragically slipped. McCabe fell into the turbulent Boston Harbor waters, and the twenty-eight-year-old light keeper's body was never found.

The lighthouse was replaced with a spark plug light in 1982. The Deer Island Sewage Treatment Plant, boasting 150-foot-tall sludge digesters, opened in 1995 and became fully operational in 2000. The facility is responsible for purifying the toxic waters of Boston Harbor.

However, the sounds of the treatment facility can't drown out the postmortem cries of the hundreds who died on the land the Native Americans called Devil's Island.

File under: native nightmare

Long Island

If there's one Boston Harbor legend that could rival Georges Island's Lady in Black, it would be the Woman in Scarlet Robes. She's often overshadowed by the ghostly theatrics of the southern belle believed to haunt Fort Warren, but Long Island's resident phantom had an equally traumatic demise.

In contrast to her made-up counterpart, the lady in red seems to be historically viable. In other words, the Woman in Scarlet Robes legend might actually be based on fact. She's a true ghost of the American Revolution, an embodiment of the chaos that unfolded in Boston Harbor on March 17, 1776.

Her name was Mary Burton, and she's sometimes still seen walking along Long Island's shoreline, covered in blood and looking for her husband. People claim to hear this wailing woman's specter begging for help.

Boston built a poorhouse and eventually a chronic disease hospital on Long Island in the 1880s. The facility, menacing by design, included a crematorium for the hundreds of sick and suffering who perished in these reportedly inhumane facilities. *Courtesy of the Boston Public Library, Print Department.*

On what the locals know as Evacuation Day and everyone else calls St. Patrick's Day, attempts by the British to occupy Boston were foiled by George Washington, who occupied Dorchester Heights. According to the diary of Abigail Adams, who watched the scene unfold in Braintree, more than 170 British vessels were in Boston Harbor that day and only 78, including the infamous *Somerset*, fled. Almost 100 British vessels carrying thousands of redcoat soldiers and Tory refugees hovered around Long Island for weeks.

On June 13, 1776, American soldiers occupied Long Island and started bombing the British vessels to force them to leave.

According to Edward Rowe Snow, Burton's husband, William, was with his wife on one of the remaining British ships. "Mary had become friendly with three other women on the day the bombardment started," wrote Snow in *The Islands of Boston Harbor*. "The first cannonball that hit the ship passed through the open port and mortally wounded Mrs. Burton. Still conscious, Mary pleaded with her husband."

Ghost lore speculates that the dying woman knew her wound was fatal and that she begged her husband to bury her on the mainland. "I know I'm to die, William, but please don't let them bury me in the sea," she said. "William, bury me ashore."

William covered his wife in a red blanket and delicately lifted her into a small boat. He paddled to Long Island and begged the Americans to let him ashore. Her last words to him, according to legend, were "promise you'll come back for me. Promise me, William."

She wanted a proper burial at King's Chapel. With tears streaming down his face, he swore he would someday return. Burton carried his dead wife onto the shore of Long Island near the present-day home of the lighthouse.

"A brief service was held, after which Mary Burton was buried," wrote Snow. The American soldiers on the island swore they would put her name on a gravestone, and the Tory sympathizer left his wife in a makeshift grave. He returned to the British vessel and quickly headed back to his homeland.

Burton never returned to Long Island to give his wife a proper burial. According to Snow, he died near the turn of the century, and the Americans on Long Island crafted a wooden headstone to mark Mary's remains. The marker slowly started to rot from the elements and years of neglect.

It's said that the ghost of Mary Burton, wearing a red cloak, walks the shores of Long Island waiting for her husband to return. In 1804, a group of fishermen claimed to have heard moans followed by a face-to-face encounter with the lady in red. "They saw the form of a woman wearing a scarlet cloak coming over the hill," Snow continued. "It appeared as though blood was streaming down her cloak from a terrible wound to her head, but she kept on walking, soon disappearing over the hill."

The encounters continued for years after the American Revolution and even the Civil War. "Soldiers stationed at Fort Strong reported other ghostly sightings while on patrol," wrote Christopher Forest in *Boston's Haunted History*. "Rumors started to spread about the ghostly vision of a woman dressed in scarlet visiting the fort. Following the war, the rumors subsided until the 1890s, when a man named William Liddell, a private on the island, spotted the same lady. She came toward him with a distinct moan forming on her lips. Eventually, she disappeared into the chilly Atlantic air."

Mary Burton's tragic death, which is unverified, is just one of many tragedies that has left its indelible imprint on Long Island's bloodstained soil. During the colonial era, Native Americans lived on the longest island in Boston Harbor. At one mile and three-quarters, its land was fertile and full of natural resources. It became a farming community during the 1640s and then a Native American dumping ground during the 1670s.

Hundreds of natives were loaded on barges and transported to Deer Island. One colony of natives was sent to Long Island, which proved to be a resource-rich alternative to what Native Americans called Devil's Island, or Deer Island, located across Boston Harbor. At least on Long Island, the decimated natives could harvest clams and fish.

During the 1800s, the island was being groomed to be a summer resort. The Long Island Company built several inns, including one in the center, which was described as "a splendid hotel, large and accommodating, constructed in the form of a Greek Cross." In the 1850s, the island boasted the Long Island Hotel, the Long Island House and the Eutaw House.

In response to the Civil War, the federal government seized a portion of Long Island Head for Fort Strong. By 1872, the hotels on the island became infamous for their illegal activities, ranging from prostitution to gambling and even cock fighting. Authorities raided the island in 1873 to shut down these so-called hotels of ill-repute.

The City of Boston purchased the island in 1882 and built a poorhouse and eventually a chronic disease hospital. A home for unwed mothers and other asylums for those disenfranchised by society were also housed on the island. The facilities, menacing by design, included a crematorium for the hundreds of sick and suffering who perished in these reportedly inhumane facilities. Underground tunnels also connected the various buildings, some dating back to the Civil War.

Dennis Lehane, author of *Mystic River* and a Dorchester native, said the ghostly grounds of the sterile city hospital inspired his fictitious asylum-set novel *Shutter Island*, which was later turned into a movie by director Martin Scorsese. "My uncle took us out to Long Island once when my brother and I were kids," Lehane told the *Phoenix*. "He started telling us how the ghosts of the most dangerous patients were rumored to still walk the grounds. Then he vanished."

Lehane said the weathered structures scattered throughout the Long Island Chronic Disease Hospital inspired *Shutter Island*'s Ashecliffe Hospital for the Criminally Insane. "My brother and I walked around, all creeped out, and then my uncle jumped out from behind a tree, which gave us both early heart attacks. I remember it was just bleak and creepy," he recalled. "And that's all I needed to charge the battery for the book—bleak and creepy."

By 1928, homeless men and eventually women were housed on the island. Other treatment facilities for recovering addicts and alcoholics were eventually added. A bridge connecting Moon and Long Island was opened on August 4, 1951. For years, caregivers and patients were transported to Long Island by boats. However, the bridge was closed in October 2014 and destroyed in 2015.

When the rusty old bridge closed, Long Island was completely evacuated. Camp Harbor View, a seasonal inner-city program spearheaded by the late

Boston's largest city-run homeless shelter on Long Island was unexpectedly evacuated after a rusty bridge connecting the island to the mainland was closed. *Photo by Jason Baker.*

mayor Thomas Menino in 2007, is now the only sign of life left on an island that was once home to hundreds. Several cemeteries are located on the island, including the former hospital cemetery, which contains the remains of at least three thousand deceased patients.

Former residents of Long Island, many of whom stayed in the city's largest-run homeless shelter, said the island was definitely creepy. When I was the editor of *Spare Change News*, I interviewed several of the homeless men and women who stayed there. Many believed it was haunted by the former patients of the chronic-disease hospital. "The only true nightmare on Long Island was being told that Mayor Marty Walsh had closed the bridge and the horrors we faced after we were carted off the island," said Cleve Rae, a formerly homeless man who recounted to me the inhumane treatment of hundreds of people forced off Long Island in October 2015.

I also chatted with young adults who stayed at Camp Harbor View. According to them, the Woman in Scarlet Robes is alive and well. In fact, the young campers' sleeping area is a stone's throw from Mary Burton's alleged makeshift grave. "I remember hearing about the ghost back in 2008," recalled an alum of Camp Harbor View. He asked to remain anonymous.

"It scared the crap out of me. I remember hearing her moan and imagining this woman, covered in blood, hovering over me," he remembered. "I was so scared I slept with a flashlight on."

File under: bloody Mary

THOMPSON ISLAND

When Boston's Asylum for Indigent Boys merged with the Boston Farm School Society on Thompson Island in 1835, no one could have known what heartbreaking tragedies were about to unfold for a handful of these orphaned children. Those enrolled in the newly formed Boston Asylum and Farm School for Indigent Boys had lost one or, sometimes, both parents and still somehow forged a hardworking community with minimal parental supervision.

Many of the lost boys of Thompson Island had nowhere else to go. A few single mothers who had signed over guardianship to the school until

Thompson Island, currently home to the inner-city youth adventure program Outward Bound, was the scene of several maritime tragedies soon after Boston's Asylum for Indigent Boys merged with the Boston Farm School Society in 1835. *Courtesy of the Boston Public Library, Print Department.*

the young men were twenty-one changed their minds and begged for their sons to be returned home, though most reports raved about the tightknit community on Thompson Island.

"That little island reminds me of the old mythological tale of Latona, who, when she had no place on earth for her to bring forth and rear up her young, had an island created for her own special uses," wrote M.F. Sweester in *King's Handbook of Boston Harbor*. "Something like it exists here, for when the boys who prowl our city streets, fatherless, motherless, forlorn and homeless, are discovered, this little Thompson Island rises as a refuge for them."

Nathaniel Hawthorne, author of *The Scarlet Letter* and the gothic-themed *The House of the Seven Gables*, went to Thompson Island and wrote about his visit to the asylum. "The boys swinging, two together, standing up and almost causing the ropes and their bodies to stretch out horizontally," recalled Hawthorne. "On our departure they ranged themselves on the rails of the fence, and, being dressed in blue, looked not unlike a flock of pigeons."

The boys built a community known as "Cottage Row" in the 1890s. It started out as a tent city and became more elaborate as the boys started creating wooden cabins to protect them from the harsh harbor elements. Aided by the school's superintendent, Charles Henry Bradley, the orphans created a miniature city with self-governed rules and even Audubon Hall, a shelter for their pets.

Two tragedies haunted the orphaned boys of Thompson and left a psychic fingerprint of sorts on the shoreline of the 175-acre drumlin in Boston Harbor.

In 1842, the farming students started making a trek by boat to Boston. Led by their director, the boys would line up and march to city hall, where they listened to a speech by the mayor. The kids then headed to Boston Common, where their family and loved ones waited. It was a rare but much-anticipated moment for the orphans to reconnect with their extended families on the mainland.

On April 29, 1842, tragedy struck Thompson Island. The boys' vessel, the *Polka*, capsized after a fishing trip to the outer harbor. According to reports, twenty-five boys drowned in the frigid waters of Boston Harbor.

"It was the worst tragedy in the history of the school," remarked Edward Rowe Snow in *The Islands of Boston Harbor*. The vessel was approaching the eastern head of the island, and the students who hadn't made the fishing trip were waiting and even cheering on their schoolmates from the shore. Then the unthinkable happened: the *Polka* flipped over and sank immediately.

"The wooden box that held bait floated free, and four of the boys clung to it, but the other twenty-three and the two men drowned," reported Snow.

"The four boys were brought to Boston by boats that had rushed to the scene. The tragedy left only half of the students to continue at the school and work on the farm."

Almost fifty years after the two dozen boys drowned off the coast of Thompson Island, a second tragedy befell the asylum on April 10, 1892. On a church trip to South Boston, the instructor A.F. Nordberg and ten handpicked boys were heading back to the island around 7:00 p.m. The vessel capsized near the exact spot where the *Polka* had sunk fifty years before.

"The eleven people clung to the bottom of the craft and waited for help," wrote Snow. "A tug steamed by, they shouted for assistance but the night was getting dark and they were not noticed."

The school's superintendent, Charles Henry Bradley, was getting worried and reportedly walked on the shoreline with a lantern looking for the boys. The survivors of the tragedy recalled seeing Bradley's lantern, but they were too far to get his attention. "The water was cold, and as the night wore on the more exhausted boys, one by one, slipped into the water," claimed Snow, adding that only two students survived the ordeal. The vessel floated to nearby Spectacle Island and authorities were informed that instructor Nordberg and eight boys had drowned.

According to local legend, that tragic April night in 1892 repeats itself like a videotaped replay of past events. According to passersby, they hear screams of what sounds like a group of boys yelling, "Help!" over and over. It's what is known as a residual haunting, but it only happens during the harbor's off-season. Sometimes, they even see an inexplicable light onshore, which is believed to be Bradley's lantern. It's said to be an anniversary haunting, which refers to spirits returning on a significant date to reenact a historical event.

Apparently, ghosts have calendars.

A friend who'd spent a few nights on Thompson Island in the 1980s told me that he'd heard what sounded like cries for help while walking near the water on the eastern side of the island. "I'm not the type to believe in ghosts, but I strongly believe Thompson Island is haunted," he told me, asking to remain anonymous. "I heard what sounded like screaming near the water. I ran to the shoreline but there wasn't a soul there. I looked behind me, and I saw what looked like the light of a lantern moving toward me. It quickly disappeared, and so did the screams from the harbor."

A bizarre accident also once occurred off the shore of Thompson Island. On July 4, 1892, a group of three men ascended in a hot-air balloon, cheered on by thousands of spectators in Boston Common. Manned by Professor Rogers, the doomed balloon also carried an assistant, Thomas Fenton, and the reporter Delos E. Goldsmith. Though he had conducted 118 successful trips, Rogers met with deadly misfortune in his journey over Boston. "As the gas bag passed over Castle Island, Rogers saw that he would soon be swept out to sea, so he pulled at the safety valve," wrote Snow. "The valve would not open. The balloon dropped like a rock."

Rogers and Goldsmith were able to swim out to Thompson Island while the boys at the asylum paddled their boat to the scene. Fenton, entangled in the balloon's net, died before he could be taken to the hospital. Professor Rogers sank beneath the turbulent waters of the harbor before the boys could reach him. Goldsmith was saved.

Today, Thompson Island is home to Outward Bound, an inner-city youth adventure program that opened in the early 1990s. The island, founded in 1626 by David Thompson, had the distinction of being a Native American trading post for four years before the Puritans settled the "city upon a hill." It's also believed to be haunted by the children who once roamed this island of misfit boys. Some say you can still hear the sounds of children laughing and, in some cases, crying as vessels pass the first island you see after leaving the inner harbor. Sometimes, you can even see an orb of light dancing on the shoreline. It's as if the ghosts of Thompson Island's past are welcoming visitors to the mysteries of the outer harbor.

File under: lost boys

Chapter 2

Charlestown Haunts

MaryLee Trettenero sees dead people. However, she's flipped the script of the whole *Sixth Sense* thing by reading the psychic imprints left behind at various historic locations scattered throughout New England. The intuitive behind the Spirits of Charlestown walking tour taps into the lingering residual energy at an allegedly haunted locale and then channels the earthbound spirits.

Trettenero, who moved to Charlestown in the 1980s, said she was standing on the steps of Harvard's Widener Library while taking classes at the extension school when she decided to leave the hotel industry and become a full-time psychic medium. "I haven't told many people this, but this is where I made the decision to go into the business," she said. "Once I left working in hotels, it was the only thing that really interested me. I started at a good time because it's so difficult now. The [psychic field] has become so competitive."

In 2005, Trettenero decided to redirect her intuitive abilities and channel the residual energy at historic locations. "My premise is if I can read people, then I should be able to go to a place and read the land," she said. "If energy from a historic event is strong, it stays there." As for reading allegedly haunted locales, Trettenero said it's a twofold process. "First, I pick up on the residual historical energy. The second thing is if there is spirit energy there, I would pick up on the spirits," she explained, adding that "it was a big experiment. I didn't know if it was going to work."

Trettenero said her first attempt at reading residual energy was at City Square Park in Charlestown. "I sat in the middle of the foundation of stones,

Charlestown-based medium and author MaryLee Trettenero taps into the lingering residual energy at an allegedly haunted locale and then channels the spirits. *Photo by Ryan Miner.*

and I started picking up on slave girls," she recalled. "I got dialogue and what it was like working back then and what it was like dealing with the proprietors. So I would visit the site, do some protection and then tune in. Another time, I picked up on a bartender, and one time I picked up on a pirate. After reading a place, I go back and do research and find that it's often so true to form. I'm finding that what I get from the fragments I pick up at a site is historically accurate. It fits."

City Square Park in Charlestown, which was originally called Market Square, dates back to 1629. Governor John Winthrop and his crew of one thousand English settlers originally set up shop there before sniffing around Cambridge and ultimately Boston. Thomas Graves, an English engineer, mapped out Charlestown and built Winthrop's quarters, called the Great House, in the area before relocating to Boston's Shawmut Peninsula in 1630. Apparently, Charlestown lacked a proper water source. On June 17, 1775, the square was destroyed when British cannon fire burned Charlestown to the ground. Trettenero said she tapped into a residual energy that lingers at City Square Park and predates the Battle of Bunker Hill fire.

"So when I picked up on the slave girls, I researched the slavery background and John Winthrop moving to Charlestown, and I found that slavery was totally integrated into society," she explained. "The last owner before City Square Park was burned to the ground was a slave owner."

Trettenero said she sometimes picks up on ghosts while researching historical sites. "A few days ago, I was at the Warren Tavern having lunch," she said, referring to the haunted watering hole in Charlestown built in 1780. "I was with a friend, chit chatting, and all of sudden the lights started flickering behind me.

She made me stop talking and asked, 'Who is that?' I stopped what I was doing and tuned into it. I could see somebody wearing a black coat, and he was severe looking. I immediately knew who it was—it was Daniel Webster. As soon as I said his name, my friend who is a colleague said that his name popped up into her mind as well."

How does Trettenero differentiate among the various spirits she encounters during investigations? "I have a sketch artist who works with me," she explained, adding that she first encountered Daniel Webster's spirit at the Bunker Hill Monument. "We do sketches of the spirits we see, and that's why I know what he looks like."

This 221-foot-high granite obelisk, the Bunker Hill Monument, marks the site of the first major battle of the American Revolution and, despite its namesake, sits on Charlestown's Breed's Hill. *Courtesy of the Boston Public Library, Print Department.*

Trettenero managed to assemble her residual-energy readings into a book format called *We're Still Here: The Secret World of Bunker Hill's Historical Spirits*, which came out in 2015. "About four years ago, I put it in the format of a book, but I put it down because it wasn't in a language that was easy to edit. I then added layers, like adding a sketch artist, and then I started working on paranormal investigations."

Trettenero, who runs the Spirits of Charlestown ghost tour, said Charlestown has many historical secrets. "A lot of my stuff is related to the American Revolution," she said. "I do know that the guy Harvard is named after, John Harvard, his original home is one of the sites that I do in Charlestown. It's not there anymore, but what I found is that it was a medical staging area. I just picked up on dialogue around it regarding clean water and arguments about who they are going to treat, specifically wounded British soldiers and people of color. Charlestown was burned to the ground during the Revolutionary War. But I strongly believe the medical staging was there before the war because there was a lot of violence before the Battle of Bunker Hill."

Regarding her work as a psychic medium, Trettenero said TV shows like TLC's *Long Island Medium* with Theresa Caputo have catapulted the profession into the spotlight. "We all like her," she quipped. "It's when they break the rules. With Theresa Caputo, a big part of her show is that she goes up randomly and reads the guy at the pizza shop or somebody on the street. We always say you can't do that. You always have to get permission to read someone."

However, Trettenero said she believes Caputo is the real deal. "When they aren't breaking a rule, it's fine," she remarked about pop-culture psychics. "Everybody works hard to make the profession credible, so you hold your colleagues to a pretty high standard so they don't send us back to the Dark Ages."

BUNKER HILL

Bunker Hill, which is actually Breed's Hill in Charlestown, has a rather mixed-up history. The pivotal Revolutionary War battle on June 17, 1775, would have been considered a comedy of errors if it hadn't resulted in hundreds of deaths. Yes, the revisionist history of the legendary battle in Charlestown is basically bunk.

"The whole thing's a screw-up," said *Bunker Hill* author Nathaniel Philbrick in *Smithsonian* magazine. "The Americans fortify the wrong hill, this forces a fight no one planned, the battle itself is an ugly and confused mess. And it ends with a British victory that's also a defeat."

While the British technically won, their death toll was 226, coupled with more than 800 wounded redcoats. The colonists, in comparison, had 115 fatalities and 305 wounded soldiers. Yes, the British won the Battle of Bunker Hill, but the Patriots' stubborn resistance became a symbol of the American resolve.

The whole "don't fire until you see the whites of their eyes" statement, supposedly issued by Israel Putnam to the Patriots, was probably made up as well. But it's emblematic of the confusion associated with Bunker Hill. When you have this sort of chaos coupled with hundreds of fatalities, it leaves what paranormal investigators call an aura of disaster. And this highly charged environment is a perfect storm for ghosts.

Out of the 2,200 British ground forces and artillery engaged in the Battle of Bunker Hill, almost half were counted in hindsight as both killed and wounded. The colonists lost between 400 and 600 combined casualties, including popular Patriot leader Dr. Joseph Warren. *Photo by Sam Baltrusis.*

When intuitive MaryLee Trettenero was interviewed for *Ghosts of Cambridge* in 2013, she talked about her residual-energy readings on Breed's Hill. According to Trettenero's book, *We're Still Here*, she connected with the spirits on the land next to the Bunker Hill Monument. She read the residual energy and claimed to have connected with a Patriot preparing for battle. The spirit talked about "rotting flesh," and Trettenero surmised that it was related to the casualties from the British warship *Lively*, which killed several Patriots with cannonballs. One soldier was decapitated while others lost limbs and three were literally ripped apart by the shrapnel.

Of course, this happened before the face-to-face combat on Breed's Hill, which meant an actual battle took place before the battle. In her book *We're Still Here*, Trettenero said she psychically replayed the horrors of that hot June day by reading the residual energy at Breed's Hill. "One by one, we are falling. We drop right in our tracks," the spirit supposedly told her. "The wounded have no distinction from the dead. We are in a holocaust. British uniforms are conveying blood."

According to Trettenero, the battle left a psychic imprint on the land. "Not all remains were removed," Trettenero wrote. "Since the British took over control of Breed's Hill, some of the fallen soldiers were buried in shallow graves. When the British left on Evacuation Day, March 17, 1776, the provincial army returned to Charlestown to reclaim the soldiers who had been buried at the site of the battle, so they could have a proper burial."

Paranormal experts believe the residual hauntings Trettenero is picking up are psychic remnants of the killings and unmarked graves left over from the Battle of Bunker Hill.

In 2009, a group of archaeologists and a Charlestown historian, Chris Anderson, located a mass grave of British soldiers beneath a residential garden near Monument Square's Concord Street. "No wonder our plants grow so well," mused Anne McMahon, a Charlestown resident, when she was told by a *Boston Globe* reporter about the mass grave beneath her rose bushes. "They're resting in peace. They're not haunting the place and we wish them well. It's all peaceful now. I guess that's what we were fighting for."

In 2009, a group of archaeologists and historians located a mass grave of British soldiers beneath a residential garden near Monument Square's Concord Street. *Photo by Sam Baltrusis.*

In addition to the skeletal secrets buried beneath Breed's Hill, there's the iconic Bunker Hill Monument, which also has a somewhat bizarre history. The cornerstone of the obelisk was laid in 1825, and famous orator Daniel Webster addressed a crowd of 100,000 there. Eight-ton granite blocks were transported from a quarry south of Boston. However, money ran out. Sarah Josepha Hale, writer of "Mary Had a Little Lamb" and a magazine editor, organized a "Ladies' Fair" that raised $30,000 to save the half-built structure. Eighteen years after the initial ceremony, an aged Webster returned in 1843 to announce its dedication.

It's common for visitors to the Bunker Hill Monument to take photos of orbs near the 221-foot-tall granite structure. But are these orbs actually ghosts from Charlestown's past?

Adam Berry, a paranormal investigator formerly with *Ghost Hunters*, told me that he's wary of so-called orbs presented to him in photos. "Most of the time it's just dust or insects," he explained. "The definition of an orb is a spherical object that produces its own light. So a real orb is created naturally by energy, or in theory, it's a spirit floating through and trying to show itself to you."

Berry continued: "If you take a picture, especially outside, sometimes the flash will reflect off dust or insects, and while they look round, they're not giving off their own light. Say that it's next to a tree and it's a real orb, the tree would be illuminated by this object. In Gettysburg, for example, I've seen orbs that give off their own light, and they are completely different from dust."

People who have visited Gettysburg echo Berry's comments regarding the difference between real orbs at battlefields and light anomalies commonly captured in photos.

Does this mean the orb photos shot at Bunker Hill are actually legit? Trettenero said she's a believer. In fact, she claimed to have had spirit encounters with Webster near the obelisk and even picked up on the residual chatter of people talking about his famous oration.

File under: battle scars

USS *Constitution*

The oldest commissioned naval vessel still afloat, the USS *Constitution*, is berthed at the Charlestown Navy Yard's Pier I in the inner waterway of the Boston Harbor. It's on a three-year hiatus starting in 2015 and is dry-docked

Featured on Syfy's *Ghost Hunters* in 2015, the USS *Constitution* is a three-masted, wooden-hulled frigate and is believed to be inhabited by the ghosts of former crewmembers who tragically died on board. *Photo by Sam Baltrusis.*

for much-needed repairs. Launched in 1797 and often referred to as "Old Ironsides" because of its uncanny ability to repel shots fired during wartime battles, the massive wooden-hulled, three-masted frigate serves as the U.S. Navy's official ambassador and is a throwback to the glory days of the War of 1812, when Old Ironsides defeated five British warships and captured numerous merchant vessels.

As a featured stop on Boston's highly trafficked Freedom Trail, the USS *Constitution* greets thousands of tourists daily and is a floating national treasure. It is, in essence, living naval history. However, this isn't a history that lies in a shallow grave. The blood of the fallen sailors that once stained the deck of the two-centuries-old frigate might have washed away over time, but the supernatural imprint of Old Ironsides' casualties of war allegedly continue to haunt the legendary vessel.

According to former crew members, the USS *Constitution* is a ghost ship. "We took ghosts so seriously on the *Constitution*," said Pete Robertson, a first-class petty officer who served aboard the ship from 2001 to 2004, in an interview with *Stars and Stripes*, "[that] unless you were a brand new crew member, you didn't mess around with that stuff. You didn't make jokes about it...You didn't even try to scare each other because people were terrified. A lot of people were terrified to stand watch on the ship."

Robertson remembered seeing objects, like a twenty-four-pound cannonball, mysteriously moving on deck despite the ship being completely still. "It was moving in ways a cannonball just shouldn't move," he said, adding that the odd motion was scientifically inexplicable.

Allie Thorpe, a former seaman serving between 2002 and 2005, echoed Robertson's experiences with paranormal activity while on board. "It would feel like there was somebody there with you," Thorpe explained. "It would feel like somebody was walking up behind you and blowing on your neck."

In an attempt to investigate the reports of alleged spirits, Lieutenant Commander Allen R. Brougham set up a camera overlooking the *Constitution*'s wheel one evening in 1955. "At about midnight, the figure of a nineteenth-century navy captain appeared long enough to be captured on film," one report claimed. "The picture shows a man in gold epaulets reaching for his sword."

Spirits on deck? It would hardly be surprising. As a major player in a series of nineteenth-century maritime battles, the *Constitution*'s shiny façade has been marred by the blood of former tenants.

Dorothy Burtz Fiedel, author of *Ghosts and Other Mysteries*, recounted a particularly dark chapter in Old Ironsides's history dating back to December 1884, when forty-three crew members became ill with fever and dysentery. Several died, including one man who was found on deck trying to crawl to the sick bay. In addition to the American naval casualties, several of the ship's prisoners of war were fatally wounded, including Captain Henry

Lambert from the British Royal Navy, who was annihilated by a musket ball and passed away from his injuries on January 3, 1813.

Fiedel interviewed former crew members, and a few talked about a haunted cot suspended by chains in the ship's sleeping section, or the berthing area known as the rack. "Apparently, some of the sailors, who got stuck with that particular rack, refused to sleep in it and slept on the floor. One sailor, who braved the rack, woke up in the middle of the night...and he beheld the disembodied head of a normal-sized man. The face was pale, lifeless looking and...the form faded out around the neck area." One man encountered a phantom falling from the crow's nest, and others, similar to Officer Robertson's account in *Stars and Stripes*, heard cannonballs rolling around on deck, even though they were all welded together.

Gary Kent, a former crew member who served on the *Constitution* in the '80s, described one late-night incident involving a residual haunting of a man dressed in an old-school uniform: "His jacket was black-bluish in color with gold buttons....I immediately noticed the blood on his face. He had blood on his jacket." Kent said the three other men in the rack also saw the apparition, which he described as "foggy, frosty and fuzzy," before it faded away.

While Kent's recollection of the ghostly sailor has lost its fear factor over time, the former officer said he is haunted by one strange thing he observed while serving on the *Constitution*: "Birds never landed on the ship....There were a lot of high places for them to perch, but I never saw one land. I was very new to ships....The old-timers, though, they thought it was very strange....It was very strange, definitely not normal."

Incidentally, Kent's account of a sailor wearing a navy blue jacket with gold buttons mirrors the image found in a photo taken by Lieutenant Captain Brougham in 1955. According to lore, the ghostly figure is a residual spirit of Commodore Thomas Truxton, the first man to command the *Constitution* in the late 1700s. He was known as a particularly harsh disciplinarian who reportedly tortured and murdered one sailor, Seaman Neil Harvey, after he fell asleep while manning the ship's deck. The murder was brutal: Harvey was stabbed in the gut, tied over the ship's cannon and blown to smithereens.

Perhaps Harvey's spirit is responsible for mysteriously moving the cannonballs on the ship's deck and waking up crew members in the wee hours of the night. Maybe it's a supernatural warning meant to protect the sleeping sailors from a fate worse than death—being tied to the end of the *Constitution*'s loaded cannon and blown into a thousand little pieces while all hands on deck watch in horror.

File under: cannonball run

WARREN TAVERN

The oldest tavern in Massachusetts and arguably America's most historic watering hole, Warren Tavern on Pleasant Street was one of the first buildings constructed after the British set Charlestown ablaze in June 1775. Built in 1780, the tavern hosted Revolutionary War luminaries like Paul Revere and Ben Franklin. Our nation's first president, George Washington, even stopped by in 1789 for some postwar reverie.

Based purely on its historic legacy, Warren Tavern should be haunted, right? MaryLee Trettenero strongly believes it is. "When we do paranormal

One of the first buildings constructed after the British burned Charlestown, Warren Tavern, located at 2 Pleasant Street, was built in 1780 and was visited by George Washington and Paul Revere. *Photo by Sam Baltrusis.*

investigations with equipment, we first ask the manager if anyone has seen apparitions," she told the *Boston Globe* in 2015. "One of the waitstaff has seen a Victorian woman dressed in black in the front room of the Warren Tavern. This is also where most of the paranormal activity registers on our devices when we do investigations."

Trettenero said the waitstaff has spotted a Revolutionary War–era man in a wig and tights from across the bar and near the porthole window. The bar manager said he has heard the sound of high heels clicking outside his office when no one is there.

As mentioned, Trettenero even claimed to have been visited by spirits while eating from the tavern's tasty pub-grub menu. She also features the haunted hot spot on her Spirits of Charlestown historic ghost tour. Dining with the dead? Yep, Warren Tavern is said to have a few spirits and not the kind poured from a bottle.

The tavern is named after Dr. Joseph Warren, an outspoken opponent of the British and a notorious hell-raiser. Almost forgotten in history, it was Warren who directed the team of Minutemen, including Paul Revere and William Dawes, to warn Samuel Adams that the regulars were coming. Elected as the second general in command of the Massachusetts forces on June 14, 1775, Warren was savagely killed three days later while leading troops at the Battle of Bunker Hill. He was killed instantly by a musket ball shot to the head. Adding to the overkill, he was stripped of his clothing and savagely stabbed with a bayonet until he was unrecognizable. His lifeless body was dumped into a shallow ditch, but his remains were identified ten months later thanks to a false tooth crafted by Revere.

Michael Baker, a paranormal investigator with Para-Boston, said he was wicked excited to check out the alleged activity at Warren's namesake tavern in 2011. "When we were asked to investigate this amazing place, our imaginations ran wild with the thoughts of all of the history-making discussions that must have been had by heroes and legends over a pint of frothy beer," he recalled. "The claims of activity at this place were what would be expected. Disembodied footsteps, apparitions of old patrons and the uneasy feelings that go along with being in the cellar."

Baker said his team followed strict, science-based protocol when they investigated the tavern. "The first thought I had when entering this place was that there must be a ton of misinterpretations," he wrote in his investigation notes. "The floorboards creaked when the wind blew and the classic tavern design of the place certainly entertained the idea that some old drunkards

Michael Baker, a paranormal investigator with Para-Boston, said his team heard stories of disembodied footsteps, apparitions of Revolutionary War–era patrons and uneasy feelings in the basement. *Photo by Sam Baltrusis.*

must still be lingering in the corners. Shadows were plentiful here, but sadly, not the moving kind."

Members of the investigation team did feel some unusual heaviness in the basement, but that could be attributed to the low ceilings and wiring. "After setting up our equipment for the night, we all found a place to sit and hunkered down waiting for any signs of activity," he recalled. "The apparitions were said to appear at a certain table and were only visible in the mirror behind the bar. Unusual, but with that in mind we were careful to play by the guidelines. A set of eyes and a camera gazing endlessly into the mirror."

In a sit-down interview with me, Baker and Para-Boston investigator Bart Smith said the ghosts said to haunt the watering hole were basically debunked. "We didn't encounter anything, but we did debunk a few things," Baker said. "One of the claims is that the bar manager could hear the floorboards creaking. We determined the heat in the building moved the boards, and it sounded like footsteps."

Smith said the team also found a legitimate explanation for the man-in-tights apparition often spotted at a table after the bar closed. "The way the mirror was set up, it was almost a perfect explanation because the reflection of a lamp could easily be misinterpreted. [Out of] the corner of your eye, it did look like a person."

Baker said his team spent hours checking out the mirror. "It did look like a flesh-colored reflection of a man in colonial garb, but it was an optical illusion caused by the lamp," he continued. "We did hear what sounded like a rattling-around noise in the kitchen that couldn't be explained," added Smith.

The Para-Boston investigators said that the team talked with the bar manager and employees about the alleged activity. The employees were still convinced the watering hole was indeed haunted. Both Baker and Smith said Warren Tavern's history alone is enough to warrant further investigation.

"I was watching the *Sons of Liberty* show on TV and they were talking about a tavern. I assumed it was this tavern because they were talking about Joseph Warren," Smith continued. "There is so much history here it's hard to rule it out."

While Baker's team carried out a sound, scientific investigation and found little to no evidence, he's not completely shutting the door on the possibility. "We didn't have any experiences but it doesn't mean there isn't something here," Baker explained. "If we had to make a guess based on our investigation, we would have to say it's not haunted."

File under: debunker hill

Chapter 3

FORT HAUNTS

Peter Muise, author of *Legends and Lore of the North Shore* and founder of the blog *New England Folklore*, said there's something mysterious and oddly fascinating about Boston Harbor's series of forts. Many of these historic structures, he noted, are in an arrested state of decay, which only adds to their spooky mystique.

"Boston has a long history and for many years was one of North America's most important port cities. The forts were built to defend the city from attacks by sea," he explained in an interview with me. "The first forts were built by the English to protect the city from enemies like the French but also probably from random pirate attacks. When the American Revolution started, the British used the forts to control access to the harbor and as shelter from the Americans. After the revolution the Americans used the forts to defend the city from the British in the War of 1812, and in the Civil War, the forts helped protect Boston from attack by the Confederacy. Some of the harbor forts were also fitted with antiaircraft guns during World War II."

As Boston's legends and lore expert, Muise said the forts dotting the islands of Boston Harbor are rich with stories, adding that a lot of the ghosts believed to be haunting the waters of Boston Harbor got their origins from real-life horrors. "Many traumatic events have happened on the islands," Muise continued. "Executions, massacres, shipwrecks, war and deaths from disease. Some people believe that traumas like those cause ghosts and other paranormal activities."

Left: Peter Muise, author of *Legends and Lore of the North Shore*, said there are many forgotten stories and a few unsolved mysteries associated with Boston Harbor's series of abandoned forts. *Photo by Sam Baltrusis.*

Below: One of Boston's most notorious hauntings centers on the ghost of a Confederate prisoner's wife who was allegedly sentenced to death for aiding in the escape of a soldier when Georges Island's historic Fort Warren served as a Civil War lockup. She's known as the Lady in Black. *Courtesy of the Boston Public Library, Print Department.*

One of those ghost stories—the legend of the Lady in Black—has taken on a life of its own thanks to the work of author and folklorist Edward Rowe Snow. "Well, the Lady in Black is the best-known ghost on the harbor islands, and local folklorist Edward Rowe Snow helped spread her legend after Fort Warren opened to the public in 1961," continued Muise. "However, there's no historic record that a woman was ever hanged at Fort Warren, so a lot of people assume that Snow created the story himself."

While the legend of Melanie Lanier—who apparently dressed as a man to save her Confederate soldier husband but ended up accidentally killing him—might be completely fabricated, Muise said there's some truth behind the elaborate backstory. "Snow didn't completely make up the legend of the Lady in Black," said Muise. "Historian Jay Schmidt notes that soldiers stationed at the fort during World War II did tell stories about a ghostly black widow that haunted the island and also mentions other ghost stories he was told himself, like a ghostly lantern that has been seen floating through the air, carried by unseen hands."

It's clear from these reports that the Lady in Black phenomenon is partly based on face-to-face encounters with the paranormal. However, the story, which centers on a southern woman who was rumored to be hanged on Georges Island, is a form of poetic license, used to explain the unexplainable. "I don't think her story is necessarily based on a real woman, but I don't think it is entirely fabricated either," Muise added. "It's probably based on real experiences that people have had. People see a ghostly figure in black and need to explain why this figure appears on Georges Island. Voila! The legend of the Lady in Black is born."

While the Lady in Black myth and other Boston Harbor ghost lore intrigue Muise, he's equally fascinated with the bizarre real-life stories that have emerged from Boston Harbor's forts. One story involved the larger-than-life rats found on Lovells and Georges Islands.

"Back during the Civil War, there used to be a lot rats on the island," Muise said. "They lived off the food refuse from the mess hall and dug their warrens deep under the stone walls. They were quite a nuisance, but the troops had other concerns. So the rats just kept multiplying. One day, one of the soldiers stationed on the island went into Boston to get a haircut. He kept his hair long (as was the fashion then) and had the barber style it with a pomade made from lard and sweet fragrances."

Muise said the soldier returned to Georges Island with a stylish new haircut. However, the man was plagued with dreams of buzzing mosquitoes while trying to sleep in his makeshift Fort Warren bed. "When he woke up,

Fort Warren was named in honor of Revolutionary War hero Dr. Joseph Warren, who sent Paul Revere on his famous ride and was brutally killed at the Battle of Bunker Hill. *Courtesy of the Boston Public Library, Print Department.*

he was shocked to find that all his hair was gone," Muise explained with a laugh. "The rats in the walls had been attracted to the sweet lard smell of the pomade, and they had devoured his hair while he slept."

Muise continued: "Their gnawing had filtered into his dreams as the sound of mosquitoes. To add insult to injury, his hair never grew back."

FORT ANDREWS, PEDDOCKS ISLAND

If the poison ivy–covered Peddocks Island looks familiar, it's because of the unforgettable cameo this mysterious outer harbor island made in the opening sequence of Martin Scorsese's movie *Shutter Island*. While the novel written by Dennis Lehane was inspired by the campus of brick buildings on Long Island, exterior scenes for the made-in-Massachusetts movie were actually shot on the 184-acre series of interconnected drumlins.

Fort Andrews, created on Peddocks Island in 1897, served as a camp for Italian prisoners of war in the 1940s. It was decommisioned in 1946 and was featured during the filming of Martin Scorsese's movie *Shutter Island*. *Photo by Sam Baltrusis.*

And, yes, Peddocks Island is as creepy as it looks on film.

When the film's protagonist Teddy Daniels, played by Leonardo DiCaprio, approaches the fictional Shutter Island by boat, he's greeted by two armed guards who quickly whisk him away into the bowels of the Ashecliffe Hospital for the Criminally Insane. Daniels passes by the weathered brick buildings of Peddocks Island's Fort Andrews, a World War II–era fort replete with weathered walls and penitentiary-style ruins. At one point, there were twenty-six buildings on the island, including a guardhouse, a stable, prisoner barracks and a fire station.

Today, only one dozen or so buildings from Fort Andrews remain. The rest, active since 1904 through World War II, were destroyed in 2011 after filming the movie. The Department of Recreation and Conservation (DCR) has painstakingly restored the structures still standing. In fact, the DCR recently rehabbed the 1940s-era chapel, which was originally built from a military kit, and created a series of cabins, known as yurts, for enthusiasts wanting to spend the night on the real Shutter Island.

Many of the visitors who camp on Peddocks Island claim it's Boston Harbor's most haunted locale.

Of course, the Lady in Black usually receives most of the attention. In fact, visitors stop at Georges Island before heading off to its less manicured, and creepier, neighbor. Located about one mile from Georges, Peddocks Island's ghosts easily rival Fort Warren's black widow. In fact, some believe the spirits on the *Shutter Island* set have an affinity for music.

Jerry McCormack, a Massachusetts State Park ranger, told the *American-Statesman* he had his most profound paranormal experience as a child while roaming the prisoner-of-war barracks on Peddocks Island. "Because his father was the site supervisor for several of Boston Harbor's most haunted islands, McCormack and his siblings had free rein to roam and explore places like Fort Andrews on Peddocks Island after dark," reported the *Statesman*. "It was there, at age 10, that McCormack says he had his first ghostly encounter. Wandering at night near deserted barracks that once housed Italian prisoners of war, Jerry and his family heard the clear, soulful sounds of a piano sonata wafting through the air."

McCormack said, "The piano man has been tapping out music since he was a prisoner here during World War II. He died trying to escape the island by swimming off it, returning for eternal night-time encores."

The park ranger was also mysteriously tapped on the back by an unseen force while exploring a dark hallway on Georges Island. When asked if he believed in the paranormal, McCormack responded: "You betcha. This is Boston."

Battalions of troops trained at Fort Andrews during World War I, and thousands of Italian soldiers stayed on Peddocks Island in a prisoner-of-war camp during World War II. They were detained in North Africa in 1943 following Mussolini's surrender to the Allied forces. The prison was not overly strict, and the POWs were given weekend passes to the North End, where they romanced local girls and enjoyed home-cooked dinners.

Matilda Silvia, a lifelong resident of Peddocks Island, wrote about the foreign gentlemen she interacted with in the 1940s in her memoir, *Once Upon an Island*. "On weekends, they rotated on a two-day pass to Boston. One group alternated each weekend from Friday night until Sunday night," Silvia wrote. "Those remaining on the island were allowed to have friends and relatives visit them on either day of the weekend. The guests were not allowed to stay overnight."

The POWs were sent back to Italy in September 1945. Many survivors of the camp said their stay in America felt more like a vacation and less like an internment. Silvia didn't recall any soldier trying to escape the island. However, there were at least three reported deaths in the twentieth century. In 1906, two soldiers capsized and drowned while paddling to Georges from

Built in the 1940s, the historic nondenominational chapel on Peddocks Island was recently restored and is now open for events, lectures and weddings. *Photo by Sam Baltrusis.*

Peddocks. In 1934, another serviceman died on Peddocks because of the harsh, New England elements. He reportedly froze to death and his remains were shipped to Nantasket.

Another mysterious death took place in 2012. A thirty-five-year-old man was on the island during the off-season and sustained head injuries after jumping on an elevator platform and then going into cardiac arrest. First responders found his lifeless body in the basement of the quartermaster building. The DCR employee on duty apparently invited a group of friends to the island, and they were drinking alcohol. "The caretakers are there to protect the investment we've made in the island and to ward off any vandals—and we do have a history of vandalism on Peddocks Island," said DCR spokesperson S.J. Port. The DCR caretaker was placed on unpaid administrative leave. The death was ruled accidental.

So, who was the piano man? Several volunteers and employees who have spent time on the island were interviewed for this book. One volunteer, who asked to remain anonymous, said he'd seen the actual piano played by the supposed ghost of Peddocks Island. "It was in one of the off-limits prisoner-of-war barracks," he said. "I also remember seeing an amazing mural painted on the walls in the prison. It looked like something you would see in Italy. It's all boarded up now and you can't go inside to see it, but I remember sneaking in one night because I heard rumors that one of the Italian prisoners painted it. The mural was beautiful." The barracks are now completely off-limits since the accidental death in 2012.

Campers who frequented Peddocks often talked about hearing piano music on the island. Other reports said the music from beyond sounded more like wind chimes. Campers also talked about spotting a grayish-colored horse galloping on the island and disappearing without a trace.

Is there also a ghost horse on Peddocks? One man said he calls the spirit animal "Smokey" and affirmed that the horse has been spotted on the island for years. Volunteers who helped rehabilitate the structures on Peddocks swear that the stable, which served as overnight quarters for park rangers and DCR employees who weren't staying in the renovated old guardhouse, is the most haunted structure on Peddocks. They've reported hearing noises that sound as if a horse is tapping its hoof and the smell of hay, even though the island has been without a horse for years.

"I've seen Smokey several times," insisted one volunteer. "He would gallop across the shoreline and then disappear, like a puff of smoke, when our boat approached the island."

Named after Leonard Peddock, who may or may not have actually lived on his namesake land, the island has a history of animals grazing its mainland. In fact, before the revolution in the summer of 1775, the British looted the island. They stole sheep and cattle from Peddocks and reportedly burned down buildings and farms on Thompson and Grape. They even stole two horses from Governors Island, which is now the runway area for Logan International Airport in East Boston.

Maybe the ghost horse is related to the hell-raising redcoats during the revolution?

Visitors to Peddocks Island swear that the stable is the most haunted structure on the island. According to reports from DCR employees and park rangers, the structure is inhabited by a horse ghost. *Photo by Sam Baltrusis.*

One theory relates to a tragedy involving Native Americans and a crew of French explorers on Peddocks Island years before the Puritans established Boston in 1630. "A French trading vessel was riding anchor off the shores of the island when the Indians massacred all the men except five whom they saved to exhibit around to the various tribes of Massachusetts," wrote Edward Rowe Snow in *The Islands of Boston Harbor*. Snow also alluded to the possibility that a colonial-era French encampment was set up on the East Head of the island, the future location of Fort Andrews. Cursed Native American land stained with blood? Sure, it's viable.

Another possible explanation could be related to nearby Spectacle Island, which for years served as a massive trash dump that notoriously polluted the harbor. In 1850, Boston-based entrepreneur Nahum Ward moved his horse-rendering facility to the island. His plant recycled the dead animals and turned their carcasses into an array of household items including glue, shoes and fertilizer. Believe it or not, Bostonians from the Industrial Revolution era dumped their dead horses in Boston Harbor.

Perhaps one of those four-legged animals found a postmortem home on Peddocks Island?

File under: horse feathers

FORT REVERE, HULL

Many over-the-top urban myths swirl around this forgotten haunt nestled at the top of Hull Village's Telegraph Hill. Based purely on its weathered, graffiti-tagged aesthetic, Fort Revere looks like a typical ghost hangout. In fact, the long-deactivated fortification is buried in the ground, and there are a series of labyrinthine tunnels and pitch-black hallways rumored to be haunted by the ghosts of its French prisoner-of-war past. Hundreds died from a smallpox outbreak in the late 1700s, and some claim you can still hear a musical requiem echoing throughout its dark and scary halls.

Fort Revere, an eight-acre historic site located on Hull, is a long-deactivated fortification and is said to be haunted by French prisoners of war decimated by a smallpox outbreak in the 1700s. Reports include shadow figures, a ghost choir and disembodied voices. *Photo by Sam Baltrusis.*

Formerly called Fort Independence and renamed to honor minuteman Paul Revere, the earthen works battery has become a popular hangout for teens armed with cans of spray paint. Messages are sprayed throughout the fort. Some phrases are nonsensical, but occasional wise one-liners like "everything is hard before it is easy" and "welcome to the jungle" greet visitors to this once formidable haunt on the Hull peninsula.

Based purely on its breathtaking views, Fort Revere is the one spot in Boston Harbor where visitors can see the four Brewster islands and the majestic Boston Light in all its three-hundred-year glory. The Hull peninsula is also a stone's throw from Peddocks Island, and the Pemberton Point ferry terminal is the closest people can get to the dock featured in Martin Scorsese's *Shutter Island* without actually taking a boat trip there during the summer.

During the American Revolution, Hull was the perfect location to view the real-life drama unfolding in Boston Harbor.

It's believed that Fort Revere was first occupied by rebel forces after the conclusion of George Washington's siege of Boston. In fact, historians believed the fort was used to fire on the British blockade in the harbor in June 1776. Until 1780, it was occupied by the French, who had allied with the Patriot militia and sent military resources and an army to help fight the redcoats. During this era, the smallpox plague decimated those housed on Telegraph Hill. Fort Revere was reactivated during the War of 1812. The weathered fort that exists today was created in the late 1800s and became one of the various reactivated fortifications in Boston Harbor during World War I and World War II.

As far as the alleged hauntings at Fort Revere are concerned, the ghost lore sometimes overshadows its illustrious history.

"There have long been reports of whispering and the sound of footsteps in this abandoned U.S. military fort that is now a local tourist attraction," reported WZLX, a CBS-owned rock station. "Shadows pass under doorways as if people are walking past on the other side of the door, when there is actually no one there."

In 2013, a reporter with *Dig Boston* filed a story called "Unoccupied Boston: Fort Revere." Kat Strumm wrote that Fort Revere is "definitely haunted by bad graffiti artists" but was quick to dismiss the ghost lore associated with this Revolutionary War–era haunt. Strumm tested out the legends that she deemed "lame" and conducted a mock investigation. Of course, she didn't encounter any paranormal activity.

"If you throw something in the tunnel, something might throw it back," Strumm recounted the legends. "If you stand still, you might see shadows with no source moving about. If you stand in a pitch-black room, of which there are many that smell like wet cigarettes and human pee, you can hear disembodied voices. Didn't happen for me."

In addition to its fortification history, the area known as Telegraph Hill was home to a communication tower built by John Rowe Parker in 1827. The first electrical telegraph came to Hull in 1853. Several other telegraph stations were built on the site and occupied the elevated location until 1938, when radio communications made the telegraph obsolete.

Anne Kerrigan, assistant director of East Bridgewater Community Television and co-host of *Ghost Chronicles: Next Generation*, told me that she investigated Fort Revere with her now-disbanded paranormal team, East Bridgewater's Most Haunted, in 2007. Kerrigan believes there might be some truth behind the fort's over-the-top legends.

"We got a lot of EVPs here, one of which sounded like a choir singing," Kerrigan said, adding that she released the electronic voice phenomena on the show *East Bridgewater's Most Haunted*. "You will hear the EVP of the choir in this episode. We also heard the usual bumps and noises that were not accountable to anything directly," she continued.

Does Kerrigan think Fort Revere is haunted? Based on her five-hour investigation in 2007, she's not completely convinced. However, she was amazed by the EVPs captured by Michael Markowicz. "As far as anything specifically paranormal occurring when we were there, I would have to say no," she responded. "Do I think it's haunted? I would have to say yes, based on our EVP recordings."

Markowicz, who was interviewed by the *Patriot Ledger* about the investigation, said he didn't feel anything hostile during the investigation at Fort Revere. However, he was surprised by the singing captured on his digital recorder. Markowicz also recorded an EVP that oddly sounded as if his name was being repeated at a low frequency.

The disembodied male voice said, "What do you want with us, Michael?"

Watching the group's taped investigation, I found several of the EVPs unsettling. One voice said, "Watch us, watch you," implying that the energy at the fort is possibly intelligent. Another voice responded to Kerrigan, on command, during one segment when she asked if the ghost was in the military. "I was a soldier," it responded. Kerrigan also conducted a pendulum session, and the pendulum responded, "Yes" when asked if any female spirits reside at Fort Revere.

Oddly, the recording of the ghost choir of Fort Revere featured a female soprano singing a few notes from what sounded like an operatic aria. And

According to a *Dig Boston* story on Fort Revere, the historic site is "definitely haunted by bad grafitti artists." *East Bridgewater's Most Haunted* investigated in 2007 and picked up several convincing EVPs, including a female voice singing and a disembodied male voice claiming to be a soldier. *Photo by Sam Baltrusis.*

yes, the ghostly opera singer was able to hit a few glass-shattering high notes. Bravo—or is it brava?

File under: singing specter

Fort Warren, Georges Island

One of Boston's most notorious hauntings centers on the ghost of a Confederate prisoner's wife who was sentenced to death for aiding in the escape of a soldier when Georges Island's historic Fort Warren served as a Civil War lockup.

According to the legend popularized by historian Edward Rowe Snow, a gun-toting southern woman named Melanie Lanier disguised herself as a male prisoner, snuck into the fort in an attempt to free her newlywed husband and managed to infiltrate his cell. When the duo were approached by Fort

The marching song "John Brown" was written by the men at Fort Warren using a melody from an old Methodist camp song. It was overheard by Julia Ward Howe and inspired "Battle Hymn of the Republic," which was initially published as a poem. *Courtesy of the Boston Public Library, Print Department.*

Warren's Colonel Justin Dimick, the wife haphazardly fired her pistol and killed her husband instead. When the gutsy woman from North Carolina was sent to the gallows, her last request was to wear female clothing, which came in the form of a makeshift black robe whipped together by Union soldiers. She's known as the Lady in Black.

Located seven miles from downtown Boston, Georges Island is one of the more popular stops on the Boston Harbor Islands ferry tour and was used as farmland before it was acquired by the government for coastal defense. Built in 1847, the island's Fort Warren is a ghostly, pentagonal-shaped granite structure once used as a training camp, a sentry post and a prison for Confederate soldiers during the Civil War. It also defended Boston during the Spanish-American War and through World Wars I and II before it was decommissioned in 1947.

The first Confederate war prisoners arrived at Fort Warren on October 31, 1861. Colonel Dimick, a West Point graduate and Mexican War veteran, anticipated housing 150 prisoners. According to newspaper reports in 1861, more than 800 Confederate soldiers arrived at the ill-prepared Fort Warren, and a feeling of "pity rather than...hatred of the visitors" was exacerbated by the distressed state of the fort. Despite the less-than-stellar conditions, Dimick was lauded for his humane treatment of the prisoners, and Bostonians rallied to help with food rations and bedding, hoping that the Union war prisoners would receive equally hospitable care.

However, the so-called Lady in Black didn't fare so well. According to Snow's story, reprinted in Jay Schmidt's book *Fort Warren*, "Colonel Dimick had no alternative but to sentence her to hang as a spy." Snow's legend recounted several sightings of the black widow apparition. Three nineteenth-century soldiers noticed mysterious footprints in the shape of a woman's shoes in the snow. In 1934, a sergeant reportedly heard a

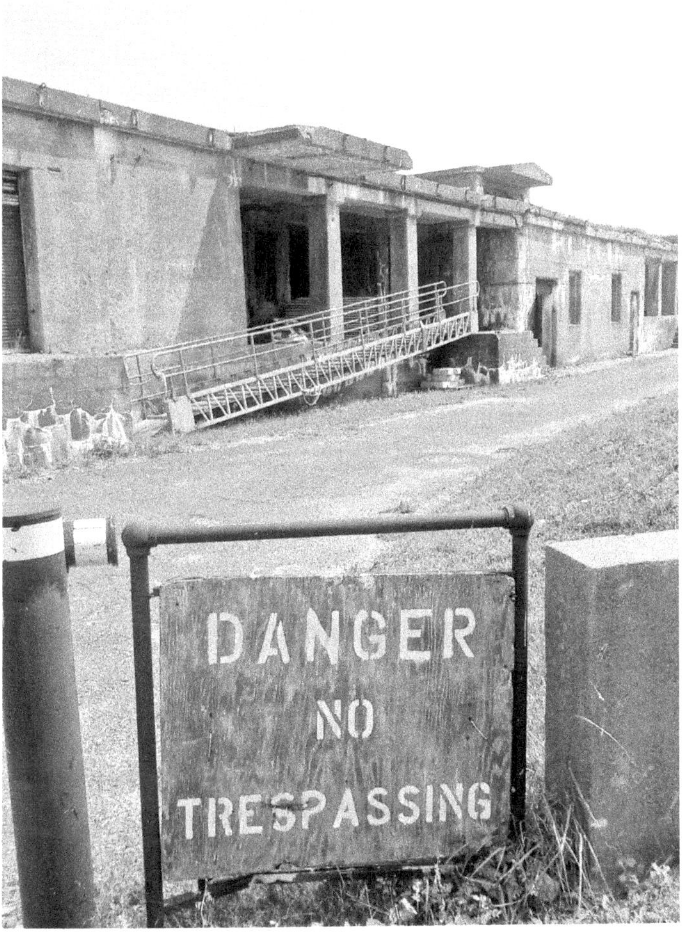

Fort Warren, made with stone and granite, was permanently decommissioned after 1950. *Photo by Sam Baltrusis.*

female voice warning him, "Don't come in here!" when he approached the fort's dungeon area. Soldiers on sentry duty shot at ghost-like apparitions and claimed they'd been chased by the lady of the black robes. Guards, stationed at the fort during World War II, would taunt new recruits when it was time for duty, telling the newbies to "watch out for the Black Widow!" The *Gloucester Telegraph*, in January 1862, reported that soldiers spotted a supernatural presence of an old woman who was "vindictively frisking about the ruins of an old building from which she was ejected some time previous to her death."

Gerard Butler, a former curator at Fort Warren who worked there during the '70s, told Schmidt in an interview that he had a few paranormal encounters while living on Georges Island. "He heard the distinctive clicking sounds of footsteps coming toward him along the ramparts," Schmidt wrote in *Fort Warren*, adding that Butler's wife and daughter were both asleep during the alleged incident. Butler also said that a police dog stationed at the fort in the late '60s was afraid of the structure's Bastion A area. "The dog would go anywhere in the fort, but once it got to Bastion A, the dog would always refuse to go inside," Butler recounted. In 1981, a crew of Civil War reenactors saw a dark shadowy figure creeping in the night and watched in awe as a lantern levitated through the ramparts without a living person holding it.

To add to the Lady in Black mystery, no recorded accounts have been found of a woman being hanged as a spy. In fact, similarly, no reports of Confederate soldiers or sympathizers being executed at Fort Warren during the Civil War have come to light.

Union soldier deaths? Yep. There were two documented executions on April 22, 1864—those of Matthew Riley and Charles Carpenter, who had notoriously joined a military unit, collected the bonus and then deserted. They were marched to the right side of the fort's demilune and fatally shot by a squad of riflemen. Today, the execution site is a picnic area. There might have been more executions on Georges Island, but the paperwork documenting Fort Warren's haunted past was destroyed when the military compound was decommissioned after World War II.

However, Butler said a crew of Massachusetts Institute of Technology (MIT) students might have conjured up the lady of the black robes in the mid-'70s. He recalled seeing a photograph shot by MIT students who had set up a camera at Fort Warren's Scarp Gallery to record paranormal activity. The former curator said that one photo strangely resembled the so-called Lady in Black. "It did look as if there was a woman apparition facing the

There's a memorial on Georges Island honoring folklorist and author Edward Rowe Snow. He's responsible for popularizing the Lady in Black legend. *Photo by Sam Baltrusis.*

camera with a sun bonnet and shawl," he said, adding that "it could have been air currents or a fog or something." Butler even mused that the photo might have been one of MIT's infamous hacks or "a mild hoax for intra-office chuckles" at the university.

Or it could have been the residual spirit of the Lady in Black taking her nightly stroll along the fort's ramparts in search of the man she murdered by mistake.

File under: black widow

Chapter 4

LIGHTHOUSE HAUNTS

Jeremy D'Entremont, author and historian for the American Lighthouse Foundation, joked that people can find at least one ghost story associated with each of the dozens of lighthouses scattered throughout New England if they dig deep enough.

"Just imagine living at an isolated, offshore lighthouse all year round, through storms and all kinds of extreme conditions," he told me. "Such an existence could easily cause the imagination to play tricks. But I do believe that many of these stories are at least partially true. Some people think that the ocean is a good conductor of paranormal energy. I'm not sure about that, but lighthouses are among the oldest structures in many of our coastal communities and their human history is dramatic and full of emotion."

Haunted lighthouses? Yes, he's heard several strange-but-true tales from the various towers. "Many of these stories seem to point to a lighthouse keeper of the past who continues to 'keep watch,' even after his death," he said.

D'Entremont, the go-to expert for New England lighthouses, said he even had a close encounter himself while giving a tour at his home haunt for fifteen years, Portsmouth Harbor Light in New Castle, New Hampshire.

"One day I was giving a tour for a married couple in the middle of the afternoon," he told me. "We were at the top of the stairs, in the watch room. I was leaning against a ladder and telling them some of the history of the place." It was the start to any ordinary tour.

"As I was talking, a low, gravelly, male voice from my right said, 'Hello,'" D'Entremont continued. "I stopped, and I asked the couple if they heard

Little Brewster's historic Boston Light, originally built in 1716, has withstood blizzards, erosion, fires, lightning, shipwrecks and ghosts. *Photo by Frank C. Grace.*

anything. The husband in the group swore he also heard a man say, 'Hello,' whereas his wife didn't hear a peep. We looked down the stairs and outside, and there was nobody else anywhere near the lighthouse. A few other people have had similar experiences."

D'Entremont has been on multiple paranormal investigations and has heard a few spine-tingling stories from former keepers and visitors over the years. "Once I was talking on the phone with a man who was a Coast Guard keeper at an isolated lighthouse in Maine. He laughingly said, 'You know, some keepers thought there were ghosts at the lighthouses.' I thought he viewed the idea as a joke."

However, the keeper's tone quickly turned serious. "One time, I was outside late at night, and I looked over at the lighthouse tower," he told D'Entremont. "I saw a woman sitting on the railing on the top of the tower. I know I saw her, but I know there was really no woman there. I can't explain it."

Of course, D'Entremont said extreme isolation could factor into each alleged ghost sighting. "I definitely think living at a remote, isolated location can play tricks on your imagination," he continued. "I have no doubt that some ghost stories were based on strange, but natural, sights and sounds experienced by the keepers and their families. I also think that keepers and family members shared stories, and they are prone to exaggeration as they're passed down."

As far as the lighthouses in Boston Harbor are concerned, D'Entremont said he's heard quite a few stories about the three-hundred-year-old Boston Light. "Dennis Dever, the Coast Guard keeper in the late 1980s, told me that his radio in the boathouse would change itself from a rock station to a classical station," the historian recalled. "He also said that one time he was looking out a window in the keeper's house toward the lighthouse tower and he saw a man standing in the lantern room. Alarmed, he ran to the tower and ran up the stairs—and there was nobody there. He told me he was positive he saw someone."

D'Entremont offers a lecture on the haunted lighthouses of New England. He said folklorists, like the late, great Edward Rowe Snow, helped shine a light on the preservation of these remote, offshore lighthouses he's grown to love. "The stories he told drew attention and inspired many people—including me—to become interested in the islands, forts and lighthouses of Boston Harbor," D'Entremont said. "I was lucky enough to meet him a couple of times, and Edward Rowe Snow was one of the big influences of my life. He was a larger-than-life character who did everything with passion."

Does he think Snow fabricated the sometimes over-the-top tales of ghostly damsels in distress and other fearsome phantoms allegedly haunting Boston Harbor? "I don't think he made up the stories, but I think he took some of them and ran with them—particularly the Lady in Black," D'Entremont continued. "In his early books, Snow stated that he couldn't guarantee that any part of the story was true. But he definitely popularized it, and it became one of his signature stories."

D'Entremont said the biggest hurdle facing the historic lighthouses in Boston Harbor has little to do with the ghosts. It's about preservation. "It's a struggle," he emoted. "I would urge anyone who cares about lighthouses to volunteer or to donate to an organization like the American Lighthouse Foundation. Every dollar helps."

The lighthouse aficionado continued: "The next couple of decades will be very telling for offshore lighthouses, especially when you add rising sea levels into the mix."

The one story that still creeps out D'Entremont centers on the Penfield Reef Light in Fairfield, Connecticut. "A few days before Christmas in 1916, the head keeper, Fred Jordan, left to row to shore to visit his family. A sudden storm blew in, and he was capsized and drowned within sight of the assistant keeper at the lighthouse."

D'Entremont said Rudolph Iten, the assistant, became the next head keeper. "A few days later, he saw a 'gray, phosphorescent figure' go down the stairs in the keeper's house. He followed, but there was nobody there. When he went to his desk, he found that the logbook had been pulled off a shelf and was open to the day when Jordan had died," he recalled, adding that Iten had multiple face-to-face encounters with the ghost of the fallen light keeper years after the initial incident.

Is D'Entremont a believer? Yes. "Lighthouse keepers had tremendously strong emotional ties to their lighthouses, so it's not that much of a stretch for me to think a keeper's spirit might choose to remain at a lighthouse or to make an occasional visit," the expert confirmed.

BOSTON LIGHT

There's an inexplicable mystique radiating from Little Brewster's Boston Light. Celebrating its three-hundred-year anniversary in 2016, it's located approximately nine miles offshore from downtown and dates back to 1716.

Boston Light, nestled on Boston Harbor's Little Brewster Island, celebrated its three-hundred-year anniversary in 2016. *Photo by Frank C. Grace.*

Boston Light was rebuilt in the eighteenth century after the redcoats torched the original structure during the Revolutionary War. It's the second-oldest working lighthouse in the country, and its ninety-eight-foot-high tower has seen almost three centuries of tragedy, starting with the death of the light's first keeper, George Worthylake, who drowned alongside his wife, daughter and two other men when their boat capsized a few feet from the island's rocky terrain in 1718.

The ghosts from the Boston Light's early days have captivated the imagination of the city's land-bound inhabitants for years. A young Benjamin Franklin, then an up-and-coming printer, penned a ballad about the Worthylake incident called "Lighthouse Tragedy," which he later dismissed as "wretched stuff" but joked that it "sold prodigiously." Boston Light's second keeper, Robert Saunders, met a similar fate and drowned only a few days after taking the job. The tower, which originally stood at seventy-five feet, caught fire in 1751, and the building was damaged so intensely that only the walls remained. The British, angry that the colonists had tried to disengage the beacon during the revolution, apparently destroyed Boston Light in 1776 while heading out of the Boston Harbor. It was rebuilt in 1783 but witnessed several more tragedies, including two shipwrecks, the *Miranda* in 1861 and the *Calvin F. Baker* in 1898, which resulted in three crewmen freezing to death in the rigging.

In addition to the onslaught of natural disaster, one keeper in 1844 set up a "Spanish" cigar factory, carting in young girls from Boston and claiming that the stogies sold in the city were foreign imports. Captain Tobias Cook's clandestine cigar business was quickly fingered as fraudulent and shut down.

President John F. Kennedy legislated that the Boston Light would be the last manned lighthouse in the country. It has been inhabited for almost three centuries, even when the tower was automated in 1998. One island mystery, known as the Ghost Walk, refers to a stretch of water several miles east of the lighthouse where the warning sounds from the tower's larger-than-life foghorn cannot be heard by passing ships. For years, no one has been able to scientifically explain the so-called Ghost Walk's absence of sound, not even a crew of MIT students sent in the mid-1970s to spend an entire summer on the island.

However, talk of the paranormal has trumped the island's Ghost Walk mystery. "It has withstood blizzards, erosion, fires, lightning, shipwrecks and ghosts," mused a report in the April 29, 1999 edition of the *Boston Globe*, which profiled Little Brewster's Chris Sutherland from the U.S. Coast Guard. Apparently, the petty officer noticed tiny human footprints in the snow while keeping the light in the late '90s. "I'm not saying it's a ghost," he said, "but I don't know. In the past, there were kids out here, light keepers' families. There were shipwrecks along the rocks.

A former Coast Guard engineer who lived on the island in the late '80s, David Sandrelli, told the *Globe* that there have been reports of a lady walking down the stairs. Also, he said that crew members stationed on Little Brewster would hear weird noises in the night but would dismiss them, saying, "It's just George," an allusion to the ghosts from the Worthylake tragedy.

Sally Snowman, who was the first female keeper at the last occupied lighthouse in the country, told the *Globe* in 2003 that she had a few "just George" moments during her stint on Little Brewster. "I won't say if I believe or don't believe in any ghosts on the island," she said. "Let's just say I've heard plenty of stories. Some strange things do happen out here, like the fog signal, which works on reading moisture in the air, going off at 3:00 a.m. on a star-filled night. That's fun because you have to walk across the island to shut that sucker off. That can be weird."

Little Brewster's mascot, the black Labrador Sammy, reportedly had a close encounter in 1999. "He would stand up, run out of the room for no reason and was shaking all over," recalled a former keeper, Gary Fleming.

"It really does get spooky. You have plenty of time here, and if you let your mind go, you can freak yourself out," Fleming said, adding that he believes in the supernatural.

Snowman echoed Fleming's comments about the canine mascot's odd nightly ritual. "He's been out here six years, and at dusk every night he barks and barks," she mused. "We call it the Shadwell Hour, after the slave who died."

So who's Shadwell? Mazzie B. Anderson, a woman who was stationed with her husband on Little Brewster in 1947, recalled hearing footsteps when no one was there and watching the foghorn engines magically start themselves when her husband was ill. She also heard maniacal laughter followed by the sobs of a female voice yelling, "Shaaaadwell, Shaaaadwell!" It turns out that Worthylake, his wife and their youngest daughter, Ruth, capsized near the island, and the eldest daughter, who was left behind with her friend Mary Thompson, reportedly witnessed her family's demise. In addition to servant George Cutler and friend John Edge, the capsized vessel included an African American slave.

According to lighthouse historian Jeremy D'Entremont, another person, rarely mentioned in the history books, was on the island that day. "The first keeper, George Worthylake, died in November 1718 along with five other people when their canoe capsized," he said. "One of the people who died was the slave. It's not necessarily well known that there were two slaves at Boston Light at that time—there was also a woman named Dinah."

Some believe the postmortem screams heard on the island belong to the forgotten African American woman who watched the horror unfold off the shore of Little Brewster. "Somehow the canoe capsized and all went overboard," wrote Anderson in the October 1998 edition of *Yankee* magazine. "The African made a valiant attempt to save all hands, but failed. The young girl was the last to go under, still calling his name. No one survived."

The name of the courageous African American slave? He was known as Shadwell.

File under: anniversary ghost

Long Island Head Light

Added to the National Register of Historic Places in 1987, the Long Island Head Light got its start in 1819 as a twenty-foot-high stone tower. After falling into disrepair and surviving a series of storms, the original Inner

The Long Island Head Light is home to the Woman of the Scarlet Robes legend. The wailing woman spirit is said to have been fatally wounded during the American Revolution and buried in a makeshift grave on the island. *Courtesy of the Boston Public Library, Print Department.*

Harbor Light, as it was initially called, was demolished and replaced three times. The second version of the Long Island lighthouse was made out of cast iron. It was moved to its current location on the northeast end of Long Island in 1901 and was recrafted in stone to avoid the wayward gunshots from the troops preparing for battle at Fort Strong.

The historic structure's light was extinguished in 1982 and then relit in 1985 after years of neglect. The Coast Guard made an attempt at refurbishing the unmanned lighthouse in 1988 but was not able to finish. Its present-day shell can be seen peeking from the thicket on the extreme tip near the ruins of the fort.

In addition to the ghostly lore involving the Woman in Scarlet Robes, which was discussed in the "Asylum Haunts" chapter, several notable stories involving the tip of Long Island have become harbor legend.

The first death at the lighthouse was in October 1825. Keeper Lawrence, a veteran of the War of 1812, sustained injuries during the Battle of Fort Erie and died inside the stone structure. However, Lawrence wasn't the last keeper to have a visit from the grim reaper while living at the Long Island Head Light.

Keeper Edwin Tarr died on January 18, 1918 "while sitting in his chair looking over the water," reported Edward Rowe Snow in *The Islands of Boston Harbor*. The funeral was held in an old building attached to the lighthouse. It was a frigid January in Boston Harbor and Snow said a sleet storm enveloped the island so that it became an "ice-coated drumlin." Tarr's four pallbearers were a bit surprised by the slippery Long Island terrain as they carried the coffin out of the building.

"Suddenly one of the soldiers skidded, the coffin went down onto the ice, and the four men were forced to grasp the handles of the coffin and get aboard as the casket began traveling down the hill over the ice," Snow continued. "Thirty seconds later the casket—which had become a toboggan—ended its weird trip down the hill at a point just near the head of the wharf."

According to Lighthouse Friends, Tarr was the last full-time keeper on Long Island. "Following Tarr's death, several custodians cared for the light until it was automated in 1929," the website confirmed. "The light was decommissioned in 1982, but that decision was soon reversed. The light was refitted with a solar-powered optic, visible fifteen miles away, and relit in 1985. Since then some necessary repairs have been performed to the tower, which is now mostly obscured by trees that have been allowed to grow up on the island."

The late Pierce Buckley, known for his work at the Boston Public Library, capsized in a canoe off the shores of Long Island in 1890. Snow said Buckley and his friend held on to the overturned vessel for dear life and feverishly paddled to the lighthouse to beg the keeper for help. "Reaching the island, they climbed up the hill leading to the lighthouse, but the keeper of Long Island Light told them in no uncertain terms to get off the island," recounted Snow. "The boys, shivering and wet, furled their sails, climbed back into the canoe, and paddled off toward South Boston where they finally arrived more dead than alive."

Because of its proximity to three long-gone drumlins—Bird, Apple and Governors Islands—the Long Island lighthouse also had a bird's-eye view of a handful of forgotten ghosts from Boston Harbor's past.

The now flattened-out Governors Island boasted what is believed to be Boston's first ghost sighting. The island's owner, John Winthrop, told the tale of three sailors who were in Boston Harbor on January 18, 1664. According to Snow, the harbor started to churn and a set of strange lights emerged from its frozen waters and the energy shot out "sparkles and flames." The sailors were understandably surprised and mortified when the orbs transformed into the shape of a man.

Snow said the water spirit tried to lure the three sailors into his underwater abyss, saying, "Boy, boy, come away, come away." Luckily, the three men fled the scene and didn't succumb to the sinister sprite's demands.

Apple Island, which was razed in 1946 to become the runway of East Boston's Logan International Airport, was home to the ghosts of two star-crossed lovers. According to Snow, a girl who was descended from the city's early governors was murdered by a group of hoodlums living on the island. "The young girl's sweetheart at once suspected that the men were the cause of his lady's death," wrote Snow. "Nothing was heard from him for weeks, until a friend finally disclosed that he had gone to the island and joined the robber band in order to find out the details of the girl's death."

Snow claimed that a fisherman spotted a lifeless body hanging from an elm tree on Apple Island. When the authorities investigated, they found it was the man who had tried to avenge his girlfriend's death. "The ghosts of the two were said to be still walking up and down the shores and around the great elm in 1900," Snow continued, adding that the spirits of the star-crossed lovers haven't been heard from or seen in years.

Bird Island, which was also absorbed by the airport in East Boston, was one of the two islands in Boston Harbor where the hanged bodies of pirates were showcased as a way of warding off potential witches, rakes and rogues. The other was the allegedly haunted Nix's Mate. One tall tale from Bird Island's past involves events that occurred during the winter of 1634. A group of men were heading to Boston after a visit to Deer Island. It was exceptionally cold, so the crew stayed overnight and weathered the storm on Bird Island. By morning, Boston Harbor had frozen over and the stranded men could walk safely on the sheets of ice and even managed to trek back to the mainland.

Meanwhile, the now vacant Long Island Head Light stands as an eerie sentinel, protecting the secrets of the inner harbor's haunted past. In 2015, the bridge connecting Long Island to Moon Island was dismantled, displacing hundreds of homeless men and women who considered Boston's largest city-run shelter their home. Camp Harbor View, which welcomes legions of inner-city kids to the island every summer, continued after the Long Island bridge was destroyed, but the program's future is in jeopardy.

"Boston may have been a beacon on a hill, but it cut its teeth by the sea," wrote Christopher Forest in *Boston's Haunted History*. "While Boston's waterways have been home to a flurry of activity, they have also been home to an array of local lore. The famed Boston Harbor Islands alone are a virtual treasure trove of ghostly tales."

Two if by sea? Because of its water-bound landscape, much of Boston's spooky maritime past has been lost at sea. However, a few ghostly tales have surfaced over the years, like long-forgotten messages in bottles from Boston Harbor's frigid and apparently haunted waters.

File under: harbor's harbinger

MINOTS LEDGE LIGHT

Haunted lighthouses for sale? Only in New England. Minots Ledge Light, located about one mile offshore from Scituate and Cohasset, was auctioned off in October 2014 to a private bidder—identified later as Boston-based philanthropist Bobby Sager—for a mere $222,000.

Lighted for the first time on January 1, 1850, Minots was built in response to the record number of maritime disasters in the southeast corner of Boston Harbor. In fact, the rocky terrain surrounding Minots Ledge was responsible for the destruction of forty vessels in the 1830s, including a heartbreaking incident involving the death of dozens of Irish immigrants en route to Boston to start a new life in America.

The first Minots Ledge Light was built between 1847 and 1850 and was destroyed by a major storm in April 1851. Joseph Wilson and Joseph Antoine, the two men stationed at the lighthouse that night in 1851, are believed to be responsible for its alleged hauntings. *Courtesy of the Boston Public Library, Print Department.*

The lighthouse's initial promise was short-lived. In April 1851, the original wooden structure was lost at sea when a torrential, nor'easter-like storm literally ripped the tower off its ledge. Designed by the Corps of Topographical Engineers, it was built to be pinned to the ledge. Apparently, the Corps's approach didn't work.

"The residents along the shore remember seeing the flashing beam as late as one o'clock the following morning, but when dawn came the structure had disappeared," Snow wrote in *The Islands of Boston Harbor*. "At low tide the jagged edges of the piling, bent and broken, were visible a few feet above the ledge. The two keepers had been lost."

Joseph Wilson and Joseph Antoine, the two men stationed at Minots that dark and stormy night in 1851, are said to be responsible for its alleged hauntings. Several websites claimed that the keepers left a message in a bottle, saying: "The lighthouse won't stand over to night. She shakes two feet each way now." Also, there were reports of what sounded like gibberish echoing near the lighthouse. It was a mystery until a group of fishermen from Portugal deciphered the postmortem warning of "ficar longe."

Jeremy D'Entremont, author of *The Lighthouse Handbook: New England*, told *Haunted Boston Harbor* that even the phantoms of Minots Ledge Lighthouse were wary of New England's notoriously capricious weather. Storms seemed to exacerbate the activity inside the dark tower. And based on regional ghost lore, Wilson and Antoine continued to keep watch even in the afterlife.

"The stories at Minots Light relate to the deaths of two young assistant keepers in 1851. The most common thing you hear is that the spirit of one of the men is seen on the ladder on the side of the lighthouse, yelling, 'Stay away!' in Portuguese when bad weather is approaching," D'Entremont explained. "There's also a story, told by Edward Rowe Snow, that one of the keepers heard a tapping in the walls that seemed to be a response to his tapping of a pipe on a table. It was noted that the keepers in the original lighthouse—the one that fell in 1851—would signal to each other between floors by tapping on a stove pipe."

Of course, the severe isolation of Minots Ledge Light might have heightened tensions in the tower. "One assistant keeper was driven mad by living in rooms without corners and another threatened to kill the head keeper. And to make bad matters worse, there were ghosts lurking about," reported folklorist Lee Holloway. "More than one keeper reported the presence of two phantom figures in the lantern room, and unexplained knocks and the ringing of a phantom bell were often heard in the middle of the night. Many lighthouse personnel swore that on calm, sunny days, if one looked at the reflection of the tower in the water, the images of the two drowned keepers would appear in the doorway."

Several historic New England lighthouses, including the allegedly haunted Minots Ledge Light, were put on the auction block recently. D'Entremont said it's a huge task to maintain these beloved beacons. "Auctioning a lighthouse to the public is basically a big roll of the dice—you don't know what you'll get," D'Entremont explained. "Dave Waller, who bought Graves Light, is one of my favorite lighthouse owners. He is extremely hard working and creative, and he's doing a wonderful job. Nick Korstad down in Fall River, owner of the Borden Flats Light, is another example of a successful owner who has opened his lighthouse to the public. But some other cases haven't worked out so well."

Boston Harbor's Graves Light set a record when it was sold at auction for a hefty price tag of $933,000. But is it haunted?

Multiple keepers of Minots Ledge Light reported the presence of two phantom figures in the lantern room, mysterious knocks and the ringing of a bell that is often heard in the middle of the night. *Courtesy of the Boston Public Library, Print Department.*

Dave Waller, the new light keeper at Graves Light, said his million-dollar investment is ghost free "despite a name that suggests otherwise," he joked. "As far as we can tell, Graves isn't haunted. No one recently working out there, former keepers or published reports even hint of it," Waller confirmed. "What makes you think it's haunted?"

Because of its macabre name, visitors believe the lighthouse somehow marked the watery graves of the hundreds who died in Boston Harbor. Located on the outermost rocks near the harbor's North Channel, the tiny ledge was named after Thomas Graves, who could have been a British admiral or a colonial-era merchant. No one knows the truth. However, the 113-foot-tall structure was featured in the 1948 film *The Portrait of Jennie*. It also witnessed one of the more bizarre Boston Harbor tragedies when the *City of Salisbury* freighter, nicknamed the "zoo ship" because of its cargo of exotic animals, sank in 1938.

Speaking of harbor tragedies, the two assistant light keepers believed to haunt Minots Ledge Light were recently honored. The Coast Guard cutter *Abbie Burgess* searched for remnants of the fallen 1851 lighthouse during an underwater excavation in 2007. The crew did find iron beams believed to support the base of the original lighthouse.

The Coast Guard also lowered a plaque into the watery abyss next to the ledge in memory of Joseph Wilson and Joseph Antoine. The plaque was attached to a five-thousand-pound stone and was sunk thirty-one feet into the bay. The bronze memorial read: "These brave men gave the last full measure of devotion to their duty to keep the light burning."

A lone musician played "Taps" as the bronze commemorative plaque was lowered into the water. There hasn't been a report of the ghostly cries begging sailors to "stay away" in years. Minots Ledge has become a local legend of sorts on Valentine's Day due to its automated light. It's now known as "Lover's Light," because the one-four-three flash is the numerical count for "I love you."

File under: jeepers keepers

Chapter 5

LITERARY HAUNTS

Jeffrey Doucette, a veteran tour guide with Haunted Boston, said interest in literary giants like Charles Dickens and Nathaniel Hawthorne sometimes surpasses the scare factor served up by the city's resident ghosts.

"The Omni Parker House was a frequent stop for many of Boston's famous authors in the late nineteenth century," Doucette explained. "When people come on my tours and they hear this information, they are fascinated by both the two resident ghosts—Harvey Parker and the liquor salesman haunting room 303—as well as the literary history of the building."

The tour guide said tourists are often fascinated with Dickens, who only visited Boston twice but left behind a mirror said to be enchanted with his residual energy. "Often at the end of my tour, guests will ask me to bring them up to the Dickens mirror to see where the famed author practiced and rehearsed before his Boston performances," Doucette said. "Have I felt any 'ghostly reverberations' from the mirror? Sadly, no. But just to know that one of the world's greatest authors stood in front of this mirror many times is awe inspiring."

Salem-bred author Nathaniel Hawthorne is also a favorite when Doucette treks down Beacon Street near the Massachusetts State House. "Hawthorne was a member of the prestigious Boston Athenaeum," he said. "Hawthorne spent a great deal of time there researching and writing."

Hawthorne was known to frequent Salem's historic burying grounds searching for literary inspiration. Apparently, he left no gravestone unturned during his stint in Boston. "Hawthorne spent a great deal of time wandering through some of

Built in 1798, the Massachusetts State House allegedly hosts a few residual hauntings, including a mystery involving a "Bride in White" apparition. *Courtesy of the Boston Public Library, Print Department.*

the burying grounds near the Parker House and the Boston Athenaeum. Legend has it that Hawthorne drew inspiration for the character of Hester Prynne from the headstone of Elizabeth Paine, whose grave marker can be found in King's Chapel Burying Ground."

Doucette said that another point of interest associated with Hawthorne can be found at the corner of School and Washington Streets. The Old Corner Bookstore storefront, one of Boston's oldest surviving brick structures and a featured stop on the frequently traveled Freedom Trail, was built in 1712 as an apothecary, office and home of Thomas Crease. The building was formerly the literary hub of the United States during the nineteenth century, and its publishing house actually shelled out royalties, which was a rather new concept at the time. Hawthorne's *The Scarlet Letter*, *Walden* and the *Atlantic Monthly* were all published at this Downtown Crossing building. Later, it became a bookstore and even a pizza parlor at one time. Also, Puritan spiritual advisor and Boston outcast Anne Hutchinson lived on the land and there held her notorious séances, which were merely spiritual gatherings, in 1635 before fleeing to Rhode Island and then New York.

The historic landmark is currently occupied by a not-so-literary burrito joint.

Doucette, who works in the finance department at a publishing house in Government Center when he's not moonlighting as a tour guide, said he was raised in a superstitious Irish Catholic family. "My grandmother was a tinker, or an Irish gypsy, and she would go to confession and then would read Tarot cards to make sure she was covering both ends of the spectrum," he joked. "I suspect a little of that tinker mysticism was passed on to me. My mother would always say people would die in threes.

Henry G. Weston, a former Massachusetts State House tour guide and veteran of the American Civil War, apparently spotted the shapes of "marble phantoms," or spectral outlines, emerging from the stone walls leading up from Doric Hall in the state house's Hall of Flags. *Courtesy of the Boston Public Library, Print* Department.

When someone passed, we made sure we left the windows open to let the spirits out."

Doucette was an amused skeptic until he gave his first Boston tour in 2009. "A kid on the tour shot a photo of me, and there were all of these white orbs near the Great Elm site," he explained. "The last photo really threw me for a loop. It was of me with a green light coming out of my belly, and I was freaked out."

The tour guide said he reached out to a psychic who told him that the green light emanating from his torso was an indication that the spirits in the Boston Common liked the way he told their stories. "At the hanging elm, many of the people who were hanged there were done so unjustifiably by the Puritans for crimes they didn't commit. If anyone disagreed with the status quo at that time, they were executed. Boston was founded by Puritans, and it was either their way or the highway—or the hangman's noose."

While en route to the Boston Common, Doucette's tour passes by the gold-domed Massachusetts State House. Built in 1798, the state capitol allegedly hosts a few residual hauntings, including a mystery involving a "Bride in White" apparition. Elizabeth Carroll-Horrocks, head of special collections at the State Library of Massachusetts, approached me at a reading at the statehouse and wanted to speak about a ghostly myth she was unable to verify.

"I found one possible column in the Hall of Flags, but it's a stretch," she said.

After weeks of research, I able to identify the original source of the legend. Henry G. Weston, a statehouse tour guide and veteran of the Civil War, apparently spotted "apparitions," or outlines of ghostly figures, in the marble stairway leading up from Doric Hall in the statehouse's Hall of Flags.

There's a mention of these "marble phantoms" in *Curious New England*. "A series of ghosts and apparitions has been appearing for years, apparently all on their own," wrote Joseph A. Citro and Diane E. Foulds. "Visitors can readily see spectral portraits emerging from veins of Italian marble on pillars and panels. There's a life-sized likeness of the 'Bride in White' with raised arms and a veil covering her long hair."

According to *Curious New England*, there's also a "Kissing Cavalier" outline and the likeness of abolitionist and poet William Cullen Bryant. Weston spent a lot of time roaming the historic corridors of the statehouse, so it makes sense that the late tour guide was the keeper of the Hall of Flags mystery. "Neither he nor anyone else has been able to explain them or why such a concentration of anomalous apparitions should appear in one place," continued *Curious New England*.

Carroll-Horrocks hasn't been able to pinpoint Weston's marble apparitions. Hopefully, I can help the state's special collections librarian solve the "Bride in White" mystery during a return visit to the seemingly haunted Massachusetts State House.

CHARLES DICKENS

There's an eerie silence when one opens the hallowed white doors and walks into Boston's Old South Meeting House. Inside, visitors can see where Ben Franklin was baptized and, more importantly, where Samuel Adams fueled the whole "no taxation without representation" Patriot war cry against British rule.

Yep, the Boston Tea Party rally was originally slotted for Faneuil Hall, but it was moved to the Old South Meeting House because it was large enough to handle the spillover masses. At the time, it was the largest building in colonial

Boston. Old South was also where thousands of outraged Bostonians gathered to protest the Boston Massacre in March 1770, in which five colonists were killed by British soldiers.

Built in 1729 by a Puritan congregation that probably had no idea that this Freedom Trail favorite would play such an important role in American history as the go-to gathering place of record for more than three centuries, the Old South Meeting House is also reportedly haunted.

During his visit to Boston, Charles Dickens stayed in what is now the oldest continuously operating hotel in the country, the Omni Parker House. A mirror, located on the hotel's second-floor mezzanine, was taken from his room and is believed to be enchanted. *Courtesy of the Boston Public Library, Print Department.*

Michael Baker, investigator with Para-Boston, organized a paranormal investigation at the historic building. Their findings? The paranormal investigation team did record an EVP (electromagnetic voice phenomenon) of a male voice saying, "Who's there?" There were also firsthand accounts of chains rattling in the lower area of the OSMH and a bizarre recording anomaly coming from the building's steeple.

Was any evidence of a Revolutionary War–era horse spirit lingering in the building, as some have suggested? Nay—or should that be "neigghhhh"? Unless the EVP was of a dead Mr. Ed. However, several visitors to the building have reported smelling hay, and one woman who recently tied the knot in the Old South Meeting House said she had a close encounter with the horse spirit.

In fact, the redcoats ransacked the building during the Revolutionary War and used it as a horse stable and riding school for British soldiers. George Washington walked by the building during the late 1700s and was extremely unhappy with how the Brits had desecrated this important landmark.

In 1842, the Old South Meeting House made a huge impression on the internationally famous author Charles Dickens. On his first night after landing in Boston during his first tour of the United States, the author eagerly explored the streets of Boston with his publisher James T. Fields. Rounding the corner of School Street and heading to Washington, Dickens let out a "scream" of delight when he encountered the Old South Meeting House. Remembering the incident years later, Fields said, "To this day I cannot tell why. Was it because of its fancied resemblance to St. Paul's or the Abbey? I declare firmly, the mystery of that shout is still a mystery to me."

During his visit to Boston, Dickens stayed in what is now the oldest continuously operating hotel in the country, the Omni Parker House. Besides being one of the more breathtakingly ornate structures in Boston, Dickens's old haunt is also allegedly one of its most haunted. Originally built in October 1855, the Parker House boasts a slew of ghostly reports, ranging from Harvey Parker himself—who passed away on May 31, 1884, at the age of seventy-nine and apparently continues to roam the halls of the hotel he built—to mysterious orbs floating down the tenth-floor corridor and a malevolent male spirit with a disturbing laugh that reportedly lingers in room 303.

Parker's rags-to-riches story started in 1826, when he moved to Boston with nothing but a pocketful of change. He saved his nickels and dimes while working as a coachman for a Brahmin socialite and built a restaurant that later became his namesake hotel. Torn down, except for one wing, and rebuilt in its present gilded glory in the late 1920s, the hotel was called the Parker House until the 1990s, when the Omni hotel chain purchased the Victorian structure.

The hotel has several claims to fame, including being the birthplace of the Boston cream pie. It's also had a few famous employees, including Ho Chi Minh, who was a busboy, and Malcolm X, who worked as a waiter. John Wilkes Booth stayed at the Parker House eight days before assassinating President Lincoln on April 14, 1865. In fact, he used a shooting gallery not far from the hotel to practice his aim before heading to Ford's Theatre in Washington, D.C.

Other haunted happenings have involved elevators mysteriously being called to the third floor—once frequented by both Dickens and Henry Wadsworth Longfellow. The hotel's ornate lifts are known to mysteriously stop on the floor without anyone pushing a button. There's also the story of room 303, which in 1949 was the scene of a rumored suicide of a liquor salesman who killed himself with barbiturates and whiskey. According to lore, the room—which is now a storage closet—is said to have inspired horror legend Stephen King when he wrote the short story turned film *1408*.

On the mezzanine level of the hotel, next to the pressroom where John F. Kennedy announced his candidacy for president, is the so-called enchanted mirror, which was taken from the author's room and is known to do odd things when guests say "Charles Dickens" three times. "This mirror is the one that Charles Dickens used to practice his orations in front of," said Jeffrey Doucette, a veteran tour guide. "Not long ago, a worker began to clean the mirror, and he kept seeing condensation appear on the glass right next to him, as if someone was breathing on it. He hasn't cleaned the glass since."

Compared to his first visit to Boston in the 1840s, Dickens's 1867 visit was a more subdued affair. Fans once again thronged the docks—this time in East Boston—waiting for his ship, but Dickens's English manager, George Dolby, had a customhouse tugboat fetch the author and take him undetected to Long Wharf. The Parker House hotel arranged for Dickens to use a back staircase during his stay, and while the author happily reconnected with old friends, he also declined many social invitations.

His performances, however, were inarguably a triumph, with his December 24, 1867 reading of *A Christmas Carol* at the Tremont Temple being a highlight. "I never saw anything like them on Christmas Eve," Dickens wrote home about the Boston crowd. He earned $25,000, an astounding sum at the time, from the sold-out tour, which encompassed eighteen American cities, but the experience left him physically depleted.

Two years after returning home, while working on the *Mystery of Edwin Drood*, he died of a stroke on June 9, 1870. In Boston, those present for his reading in the Tremont Theatre had heard his final goodbye to a city that had become a "memorable and beloved spot" for him. "Ladies and Gentlemen—I beg most earnestly, most gratefully, and most affectionately to bid you each and all farewell."

File under: Dickens's reflection

Nathaniel Hawthorne

Did local Nathaniel Hawthorne, author of the classics *The Scarlet Letter* and *The House of the Seven Gables*, believe in ghosts? Based on the themes he explored in his books, the iconic author might have, but he definitely had a healthy dose of skepticism.

His friend William Baker Pike worked with Hawthorne at the Salem Custom House in the 1840s. Pike, a Swedenborgian spiritualist, strongly believed in

Nathaniel Hawthorne, author of *The Scarlet Letter* and *The House of the Seven Gables*, had a close encounter with the ghost of Dr. Thaddeus Mason Harris while he was a writer in residence at the Boston Athenaeum. *Courtesy of the Boston Public Library, Print Department.*

the idea of communicating with the dead. However, the author initially had his doubts. "Hawthorne was a skeptic, but he treated Pike's belief with respect," wrote Margaret Moore in *The Salem World of Nathaniel Hawthorne.*

In fact, Hawthorne wrote about his skepticism in a letter to Pike dated July 24, 1851: "I should be very glad to believe that these rappers are, in any one instance, the spirits of the persons whom they profess themselves to be; but though I have talked with those who have had the freest communication, there has always been something that makes me doubt."

While Hawthorne was initially a skeptic, he started to explore the possibility of the existence of spirits in his fiction. His book *The House of the Seven Gables* hinted at the supernatural, with one character, Alice Pyncheon, being driven mad by a spell and dying from shame. Her spirit haunted the gabled house. Also, the building's original owner, Matthew Maule, makes a postmortem return to his ancestral dwelling in the novel.

Hawthorne's skeptical tune changed later in his life. In a story written in hindsight and published posthumously, the author claimed that he had a close encounter with a haunting while hanging out at the Boston Athenaeum, a members-only research facility considered to be the nation's oldest library, founded in 1807. It was a private gentleman's club, hosting luminaries like Henry Wadsworth Longfellow, Henry David Thoreau and, of course, Hawthorne, who read books and shared ideas.

Yes, it was a gentleman's club—no, not that kind of gentleman's club.

According to his published account *The Ghost of Doctor Harris*, the famed writer in residence was eating breakfast one morning at the library's former Pearl Street location when he noticed a familiar face reading the *Boston Post*. It was Dr. Thaddeus Mason Harris, a well-known Unitarian clergyman from Dorchester, sitting in his usual chair in front of the library's second-floor fireplace. Hawthorne didn't bother the old patriarch. However, he was shocked to learn later that night that the Athenaeum regular had passed away.

Hawthorne returned to the Athenaeum the following day and noticed, completely in shock, Harris sitting at his usual spot and reading the newspaper. Yep, Hawthorne spotted the deceased doctor, looking "gaseous and vapory," and he was completely dumbfounded.

According to lore, Hawthorne spotted Harris's ghost for six weeks, and he later told his editor that he wished he had confronted the apparition. He wanted to ask him, "So, what's it like to be dead?" or at least find out if the old man knew he had passed. In fact, Hawthorne joked with his editor about the Harris encounter, saying, "Perhaps he finally got to his obituary and realized he was dead."

When the library moved to its current posh 10½ Beacon Street location across from the Massachusetts State House in 1847, Harris's ghost reportedly followed the Athenaeum's antiquarian books and his own nineteenth-century portrait. In fact, Harris's misty apparition has been spotted waiting to take the elevator to the structure's top floor.

"Most people believe this to be the ghost of the reverend that Hawthorne saw many years ago," remarked Christopher Forest in *Boston's Haunted History*. "The library was moved from that Pearl Street location to the present-day location near the Boston Common decades ago. However, it would appear that didn't stop the dear Reverend Harris from following the books and moving to the new library. Many people think Harris still rides an elevator to the third floor, so many years after he last visited the old building."

The Boston Athenaeum now opens its red door to the public in guided tours. However, the so-called haunted elevator is off limits to visitors, wrote *Ghosts of Boston Town* author Holly Nadler.

"The public is barred from using the haunted elevator, which rises and falls of its own accord as if prankish spirits amuse themselves by flitting in and out of the cabin, pushing buttons for all five floors," Nadler mused. "According to Boston ghost hunter Jim McCabe, thousands of dollars have been poured into fixing the elevator's unending glitches, to no avail."

In 2002, the Athenaeum bought a brand-new elevator, and it's still acting up. Recent visitors who toured the library contend that the lift still has a mind of its own.

File under: Hawthorne's haunt

EDGAR ALLAN POE

Edgar Allan Poe had a love-hate relationship with his hometown. The author, who notoriously didn't like Boston, was born in the Bay Village and died in Baltimore, at age forty, in October 1849. In the late 1980s, a local cab driver and Poe enthusiast was dead set on marking the spot where Poe was born. He decided to create a bronze plaque, made it himself and bolted it to the building now occupied by the not-so-scary burrito joint Boloco on the corner of Boylston Street and Charles Street South across from Boston

Boston-born author Edgar Allan Poe was honored with a commemorative statue on the corner of Boylston Street across from the Boston Common. *Photo by Sam Baltrusis.*

Common. The plaque says it was placed by the Edgar Allan Poe Memorial Committee, which has only one member—the acerbic cab driver.

While Baltimore, his final resting place, seems to have claimed him as its own, Boston has embraced its "Poe-ness" and erected a memorial statue, unveiling it in October 2014, around the corner from his birthplace. The square has become a major attraction honoring the author of "The Raven" and "The Tell-Tale Heart."

Poe was born in Boston on January 19, 1809. The offspring of two actors, the young Poe was sent to Virginia after his mother died and his father abandoned him.

He returned to the city of his birth in 1827 under financial duress. By the age of eighteen, Poe had amassed a considerable gambling debt. To raise funds and avoid his debt collectors, he joined the army under the fake name "Edgar A. Perry." Because he was too young to enlist, Poe lied and said he was twenty-two years old. Much to his chagrin, the soon-to-be-author's regiment was sent to Boston.

Poe was stationed at Fort Independence on South Boston's Castle Island. While he reportedly wasn't happy with the homecoming, the Boston Harbor fort might have been inspiration for one of Poe's most popular stories.

According to Peter Muise, author of *Legends and Lore of the North Shore*, Poe was looking for inspiration. "One day Poe noticed a gravestone in the fort's cemetery for a Lt. Robert Massie, who had died on December 25, 1817," Muise recalled in a column for *Spare Change News*. "After Poe commented on the misfortune of dying on a holiday, one of his fellow soldiers told him the tragic story behind Massie's death."

Massie was well liked by his peers at Fort Independence. However, one of his fellow officers, Gustavus Drane, had it in for the new recruit. Drane, an expert swordsman, argued with Massie over a card game on Christmas Eve. Drane challenged him to a duel and killed Massie on December 25, 1817.

"The enlisted men were outraged, and as they dug Massie's grave they quietly plotted how to avenge his death," continued Muise. "A few nights after the duel they put their plan into action. First, they invited Drane to come drink with them. Once he was heavily inebriated they led him to an unused alcove inside the fort and chained him inside. Finally, they walled up the alcove with bricks, sealing Drane inside forever."

According to lore, Poe was inspired by this real-life gruesome tale of revenge. Poe was discharged from Fort Independence in 1829, and the buried-alive story involving Drane was believed to be inspiration for his 1846

Castle Island's Fort Independence in South Boston is on the shore of Boston Harbor and has been the site of a fortification since 1634. *Courtesy of the Boston Public Library, Print Department.*

classic "The Cask of Amontillado," in which a man takes revenge on his drunken friend over an insult and ultimately entombs him alive.

Is the legend true? Muise said Poe did serve at Fort Independence, but there is some debate about what really happened between Massie and Drane. A plaque at Fort Independence supposedly inspired Poe to dig for the backstory. Massie's remains were moved from Boston and reburied in Fort Devens. "It does appear that Massie was actually killed by Drane, but his killer was not entombed alive," continued Muise. "Instead Drane avoided a court martial, moved to Philadelphia, and got married. He died in 1846 at the age of 57."

However, a crew of Brown University archaeologists did find the remains of two charred human skeletons in the early 1900s. Also, folklorist Edward Rowe Snow claimed that a skeleton wearing a military uniform buried in the bowels of Fort Independence was found in 1905.

In *The Islands of Boston Harbor*, Snow also wrote that Castle Island was cursed. According to pre–Revolutionary War legend, an English gentleman lived on the island with his daughter. The daughter had two suitors: One was British and had been picked by her father, and the other was a colonist.

She was smitten with the American boy, and the British man, enraged, challenged his competition to a duel. The Brit won, killing the young local. In a true *Romeo and Juliet* twist, the girl is said to have committed suicide in response to her lover's death. "The British officer, heartbroken, rushed down to the dock and plunged into the channel, crying he would put a curse on all who ever came near the island," wrote Snow. "Some sailors still believe that many shipwrecks near the Castle are to be blamed on this curse."

Snow said Castle Island was known for its bizarre suicides, including a man who jumped to his death in 1903 and a Somerville man who shot himself in the head in one of Fort Independence's casemates.

Castle Island is also known for its sea serpent sightings. "They were seen in 1819, 1839 and 1931," added Muise. "There were a lot of sea serpent sightings off the North Shore, particularly in the nineteenth century, but sadly only a few have been seen in the Harbor. Maybe it was just too busy or too polluted to sustain giant sea monsters?"

As far as Edgar Allan Poe's ghost is concerned, it's said that the Bostonian opted to haunt his former home in New York City's West Village. The 85 West Third Street location was where Poe penned the final draft to his classic "The Raven" as well as "The Cask of Amontillado."

New York University's Furman Hall has taken over the historic West Third Street location. The three-story building where Poe lived for eight months from 1844 to 1845 was torn down in 2001.

All that remains is the façade of his former brownstone and what some say is the Boston-bred icon's ghost. There's a lamppost in front of the allegedly haunted structure and according to the website *Curbed*, "Poe's ghost has been seen climbing it by spooked law students."

Has his ghost been spotted recently? According to multiple sources the answer is, well, "nevermore." Maybe the literary icon's spirit has returned to Boston?

File under: Poe's homecoming

Chapter 6

Nightlife Haunts

Boston's historic waterfront boasts a motley crew of nightlife locales rumored to be stomping grounds for spirits and not just the kind that come in a chilled martini glass. The list includes a bevy of waterfront haunts, ranging from James "Whitey" Bulger's old hangout in South Boston to a local pub with a secret involving a horrific death caused by heavy machinery. Apparently, the living aren't the only things that go bump in the nightlife.

Why haunted bars and restaurants? Joni Mayhan, author of *Dark and Scary Things*, told me that spirits flock to familiar places. "Bars and restaurants are places where people feel comfortable. It's where they spend some of their happiest moments, which is why it makes sense that they would also be haunted," Mayhan explained. "Spirits often return to the places where they remember happiness, hoping to reclaim some of the emotions they once felt."

Mayhan continued: "Another reason why bars and restaurants might be haunted lies in the reservoir of energy contained inside. Heightened emotions, such as joy and pleasure, produce tremendous bursts of energy, something earthbound entities require. They will often flock to places where energy is prevalent in hopes of refueling themselves."

Joe "Jiggy" Webb, host of the weekly radio podcast *Paranormal Hood*, agreed with Mayhan. "A restaurant or bar might be haunted by the spirits of former customers who frequented the establishment," he said. "They may have grown attached to the bar and spent a lot of time there or even just enjoyed the atmosphere. It may have been their spot to get away and escape."

Joe "Jiggy" Webb, lead paranormal investigator and mastermind behind the weekly radio podcast *Paranormal Hood*, wants to give a voice to those traditionally marginalized on paranormal-themed TV shows like *Ghost Adventures*. *Photo by Ryan Miner.*

Webb continued, "It's possible that the spirit could have been attracted to someone working there and returns to see that person. Also, the spirit may be captivated by all of the new faces."

As a paranormal investigator, Webb makes a concerted effort to give a voice to those historically marginalized by the major-network mainstream, which is dominated by shows like Syfy's *Ghost Hunters* and the Travel Channel's *Ghost Adventures*.

Webb said his interest in the paranormal was ignited after a series of near-death experiences, or "NDEs," as he calls them. "I was always into it, but it just seemed so abnormal," he said. In 2003, he was shot in the leg and later that year walked away from a totaled car with just a bruise. However, it was his recent brush with mortality in 2006 that opened his so-called third eye. "I had a brain aneurysm that burst, and I ended up having brain surgery," he said. "It was extremely profound. It was so profound that I came back a different person. My beliefs, my understanding, my thought processes weren't the same."

Webb, who operates a security firm during the day, said he immersed himself in all things paranormal after the surgery. "People think you're crazy when you start talking outside of the box," he mused. "But when your brain explodes and you're trying to explain it to somebody else, it isn't the easiest thing. So I started coming out of my shell and began talking to people about it."

Webb's plan of attack? "They always go to the same places and do the same things on these shows," he said. "Branch out. Do something original. There are so many things out there that haven't been explored."

In addition to hosting his weekly *Paranormal Hood* podcast, Webb moonlights as a bouncer at several nightlife locales, including the allegedly haunted Brandy Pete's in Boston's financial district. "Based on my investigation, I believe the spirit in Brandy Pete's is a male," Webb told me. "He seems to be triggered by women."

Brandy Pete's, a bi-level watering hole established in 1933, was founded by Peter Sabia. According to the *Telegraph* in 1994, Sabia "had been known for his generosity among the regulars at Brandy Pete's." The family lost the establishment in 1991 after Sabia's grandson claimed bankruptcy.

Webb believes the spirit haunting Brandy Pete's may be its namesake. "There is at least one spirit there," he said. "Based on our investigation, it seems like the spirit has some attachment to the bar and it's possibly a former worker or patron who was known by the staff. It's also possibly the bar's namesake."

Webb said the ghost seems to be interested in the bar's operations and might be attempting to manage the nightlife haunt from the great beyond. "One former female employee said the spirit enjoys interacting with the staff," Webb said. "However, some of the employees are frightened by the encounters even if the spirit means no harm."

Patrick Lyons, the restaurant's manager, said several female employees described the spirit as flirtatious. Lyons said it's common for someone to place a drink order when no one is there. He also said there have been reports of disembodied taps on the shoulder and objects like stemware or plates mysteriously moving without explanation.

Yes, Brandy Pete's resident spirit seems to have a way with the ladies, even in the afterlife.

NED DEVINE'S

Originally built in 1742, the hallowed halls of Faneuil Hall has seen its share of Boston history, including the early meetings to plan the "tea action," better known as the Boston Tea Party, and the establishment of the Committee of

Ned Devine's, a popular Irish pub and restaurant in Faneuil Hall's Quincy Market, faces Boston Harbor and is rumored to be one of the city's most haunted places. *Photo by Sam Baltrusis.*

Correspondence. The structure's gilded grasshopper weathervane, made out of copper and believed to be modeled after a similar design for the London Royal Exchange, includes a time capsule from Boston's past and boasts old coins, newspaper clippings and secret messages from former mayors.

Faneuil Hall was waterfront property until the 1800s, when Bostonians filled in the harbor in a process known as "wharfing out." The landmark was expanded in 1826 to include Quincy Market. The first open-air market in the country is now home to many shops, restaurants, pushcarts and street performers.

Ned Devine's, a popular Irish pub and restaurant in Faneuil Hall's Quincy Market, faces Boston Harbor and is believed to entertain a ghost or two. "Considering the bar's location in the historic Quincy Market and the history that goes along with that, it's no surprise," reported the website *BostInno* in 2014. "According to Ned's staff, they've had everything from moving salt and pepper shakers on tables to sightings of ghost-like images in the club and basement. An apparition rolling a barrel down the hall has also been seen haunting the bar."

The *Boston Globe* confirmed the rumors in 2015. "In Boston, you've got to have at least one haunted Irish bar. Ned Devine's in Faneuil Hall is the chosen one," reported the *Globe*. A restaurant spokesperson said that "some of the staff and management have claimed to hear voices and see a colonial woman spirit at night."

After spending several spirited lunches at the alleged haunt, *Haunted Boston Harbor* heard stories of a woman wearing period garb in the pub's dancefloor area and one waitress swore she heard horrific screams—as if someone was in extreme pain—in the bar's club area. Why would staffers report these tortuous cries from beyond?

After doing some research, I learned that Ned Devine's is in the spot formerly occupied by Ames Plow Company, which sold tractors and farming equipment. "From 1862 to 1909 the rooms in the wings of Quincy Hall were devoted to the sale of agricultural implements by the Ames Plow Company," reported the City of Boston's landmark commission report in 1975. "In 1913, this upper level was subdivided into twenty-two offices by the Ames Plow Company. The attic space held lockers which were rented out by the market's grocers and butchers."

A source who wished to remain anonymous told me that the screams might somehow be related to its Ames Plow past. "Someone probably got caught in the equipment and was screaming," he continued.

Based on a horrific death in 1907, the theory might be a viable explanation for the screams of pain heard by Ned Devine's staff. According to a police report from September 19, Victor Hendrickson from Worcester died instantly while messing with the agricultural equipment at Faneuil Hall's Ames Plow Company. "Hendrickson was adjusting a nut on a stay rod, working on a ladder, with another person holding the ladder at the bottom. In some way, his coat caught the coupling on the shaft of his right side, throwing him around the shaft," Boston's police chief reported in 1907. "He

Ned Devine's in Quincy Market is in the spot formerly occupied by Ames Plow Company, which sold tractors and farming equipment. *Courtesy of the Boston Public Library, Print Department.*

was killed instantly. His body swung around on the coupling until the power was stopped. The shafting was fourteen inches distant from the ladder on which he was working."

Based on the research of famed paranormal investigators like the late, great Dr. Hans Holzer, it's common for spirits who have died accidentally to stick around. Some believe the ghost at Ned Devine's may be what is known as a "stay behind."

Holzer, in an interview with GhostVillage.com in 2005, explained this phenomenon. "'Stay behinds' are relatively common," he said. "Somebody dies, and then they're really surprised that all of a sudden they're not dead. They're alive like they were. They don't understand it because they weren't prepared for it. So they go back to what they knew most—their chair, their room, and they just sit there. Next, they want to let people know that they're still 'alive.' So they'll do little things like moving things, appear to relatives, pushing objects, poltergeist phenomena, and so on."

Reports of a barrel mysteriously rolling in Ned Devine's bar area and the inexplicable moving of salt and pepper shakers at the restaurant is typical poltergeist behavior and is generally attributed to so-called stay behind ghosts.

What about the woman wearing period garb who's also been spotted by Ned Devine's staffers? The history pre-dating Faneuil Hall needed to be explored to uncover the backstory of the ghostly woman. "The Hall was built on top of a landfill that covers what used to be the old Town Dock, which served as Boston's port, center of commerce and city meeting place in the seventeenth and eighteenth centuries," reported the *Archaeology News Network*.

Sean Hennessey, a spokesperson with the National Park Service, said the area also has a dark history that is often overlooked. "Colonists held slave auctions right next to where Faneuil Hall was built," Hennessey explained to *Archaeology News Network*. "Ironically, Peter Faneuil, the wealthy merchant and benefactor of Faneuil Hall, was involved in the slave trade. The 'Cradle of Liberty,' as the Hall is often called due to the revolutionary activities that took place there, was actually built from funds derived from the slave trade."

Joni Mayhan, author of several books on the paranormal, including *Dark and Scary Things*, said the male energy at the restaurant could have ties to Faneuil's human-trafficking past. "If he was a slave trader, he might feel a sense of guilt for what he did," Mayhan told me. "Religion teaches us that bad people go to hell, so it's possible he's worried about the ramifications of crossing over. Or he could just be an angry bastard who wants to hang around so he can wreak more havoc on the living."

The colonists imported slaves from West Africa to the West Indies in 1644, but it wasn't until 1676 that the African-trade operation was considered successful. By 1676, Boston ships pioneered a slave trade to Madagascar and then inhumanely sold human cargo to Virginians in 1678. If they couldn't sell these human beings due to illness or gender, the Puritans brought the undesirables back to New England, and they were allocated to local families. In fact, famed poet and slave Phillis Wheatley came to Boston and was most likely sold in the former Town Dock area near present-day Faneuil Hall.

So, what about the girl ghost? Perhaps the female spirit spotted by staffers at Ned Devine's is also related to Boston's sadistic past. According to reports, the full-bodied apparition of the woman seen peeking around the corners of the two-floor restaurant looks terrified.

Mayhan said the horrors of Boston's slave trade might have carried over into the afterlife. "If the traders still have control of them, they might have forced them to stay," Mayhan continued, adding that the theory saddens her but she's seen evidence of it at other haunted locations with a history of slavery. "It's so tragic. Living a life of fear and then reliving it for an eternity in the afterlife."

File under: Faneuil's phantoms

THE MAIDEN

Human monsters once roamed here. The Maiden, a posh new gastropub located at 28 West Broadway in South Boston, had a past life as a mobster hangout for the likes of James "Whitey" Bulger and Stephen "The Rifleman" Flemmi. Triple O's received the nickname the "Blood House of South Boston" and rightfully so.

Bulger and Flemmi reportedly made decisions at Triple O's as to whom they were going to kill or shake down next. Also, there was at least one gang-style murder at the watering hole.

Louis Litif, a cocaine-addicted bookie who ran around with Bulger during his Winter Hill days, angered the Irish mob boss one night in 1982 and was found brutally murdered the following week. "Louis Litif...made the worst decision of his life in 1980 when he stopped by Triple O's bar, a notorious mob hangout, to talk with Bulger about some missing bookkeeping money that Bulger suspected Litif was using to buy cocaine," wrote Beverly Ford and Stephanie Schorow in *The Boston Mob Guide*. "Even worse, Litif was refusing to pay Bulger a cut of his trafficking profits and murdered two people without Bulger's permission. It wasn't long before Litif's dead body was wrapped in plastic, hauled out the back door and placed in the trunk of a car, only to be discovered days later at another location."

According to Brian Halloran, a South Boston drug dealer who dropped off Litif at Triple O's that fateful night in May 1982, Bulger stabbed the bookie with an ice pick and then shot Litif to death at the bar. Halloran, who ratted out Bulger to authorities, was murdered outside Anthony's Pier 4 Restaurant overlooking Boston Harbor, as was Michael Donahue, a construction worker with no ties to the gang.

It's believed that Litif was killed upstairs at Triple O's. Apparently, Bulger had an affinity for the second floor. "He liked the ambience of a second-floor room upstairs—its grit and darkness were good for shakedowns, murder plots and meetings with the nascent IRA," reported the *Boston Phoenix*.

Kevin Weeks, a bouncer at Triple O's and prolific gangster, discussed the murder in his book *Brutal: My Life in Whitey Bulger's Irish Mob*. "Strangely

The Maiden, located at 28 West Broadway in South Boston, was formerly Triple O's, a watering hole frequented by notorious mobster James "Whitey" Bulger. *Photo by Sam Baltrusis.*

enough, Jimmy, told me, 'Louie's last words to me were a lie.' Apparently, Louie had insisted that he'd come by himself and that nobody had driven him over," wrote Weeks. "It was hard to figure out why Louie lied to Jimmy that night. If he'd told Jimmy that someone had driven him, he might have gotten a pass. But it wouldn't have lasted long, since Jimmy had no intention of letting Louie run wild."

The South Boston watering hole had a history of violence long before Bulger set up court at Triple O's. In the 1960s, 28 West Broadway was called Transit Café, headquarters for the Killeen gang known for loansharking. It was during this era that the Killeen leader bit off a rival gang member's nose and spat it out before returning inside to celebrate. By the 1980s, the place had reopened as Triple O's, named for the three O'Neil brothers who ran it.

In 2007, the roughneck bar was the scene of a fatal stabbing motivated by a spilled drink. A twenty-six-year-old Revere man, Adam Rich, died from multiple stab wounds to the chest and stomach after he was attacked at the bar on West Broadway. It was then called the Six House, and the perpetrator was identified as Bernard Piscopo.

South Boston has changed dramatically since the senseless slaying in 2007. The neighborhood has gentrified in recent years and the former Triple O's has been transformed into a series of restaurants, including a sushi joint called Owl Station and most recently the Maiden.

Rachel Hoffman, investigator with the all-female crew Paranormal Xpeditions, investigated the location in 2010 and said the nightlife hot spot is Southie's most haunted.

"In the basement of the Old Triple O's, you can smell gunpowder," Hoffman told me. "For me, it's the most haunted location I have ever been to. Pots and pans crash. Nothing moves, but you hear the crashing noises."

Hoffman, who has been featured on Syfy's *Paranormal Challenge* and the Bio Channel's *My Ghost Story*, said there are skeletal secrets in the building's basement. "There's a drain down there that I believe they used to rinse blood," she said. "I heard what sounded like a body being dragged down the stairs. It made a thud noise and I caught it on camera."

Hoffman revisited the location when it was Owl Station and said she interacted with the former owner's daughter. "The place had since become a sushi restaurant. I went in last year and the daughter of the owner exclaimed, 'I knew it was haunted…they all called me crazy!' They have renovated since the opening but there are some things you can never change."

The paranormal investigator and sensitive said she had a psychic vision during the investigation that continues to haunt her. "The vibration is still with me," she emoted. "I saw a mummified head in the basement, and it looked to be a young boy with blond curly hair or maybe red. It stays with me."

Hoffman said recent renovations and fresh paint can't wash away the Maiden's bloodstained history. "I've never heard accounts to back up what I saw, so I never published that experience," she continued. "But I do know that Bulger paid off parents in Southie to keep their mouths shut."

File under: Bulger's basement

UNION OYSTER HOUSE

History oozes from the wood-paneled walls of the oldest continuously operating restaurant in the United States, the Union Oyster House, which originally opened in 1826. Before serving bivalves by the dozen and tall tumblers of brandy to nineteenth-century luminaries like Senator Daniel Webster, who came to the restaurant's U-shaped mahogany oyster bar almost daily, it was an eighteenth-century dry goods store and home to

President John F. Kennedy, when he was a senator and congressman, would dine on the second floor of the Union Oyster House, reading the Sunday newspaper and eating lobster soup. *Photo by Sam Baltrusis.*

Isaiah Thomas's *Massachusetts Spy*, an anti-British tabloid that mobilized the rebellious Patriots in the years leading up to the Revolutionary War. Louis Philippe, former king of France, who was in exile after the revolution in his country, rented out the upstairs quarters in 1797, using the fake name of Duc de Chartres and giving French lessons to young women.

The Georgian-style structure located at 41–43 Union Street is so old that the original building, dating back to 1714 and erected a quarter of a century before Faneuil Hall, was waterfront property overlooking the Boston Harbor. Fishermen would maneuver their boats within a few feet of the oyster bar to deliver their catch of the day. America's first female server, Rose Carey, worked there in the early 1920s, and there's a photo of the waitress on the stairwell wall. Owners of the restaurant introduced the toothpick to America in 1890, getting the idea from the natives in South America. President John F. Kennedy, when he was senator and congressman, would dine on the second floor of the Union Oyster House, reading the Sunday newspaper and eating lobster soup. There's a gold plaque bearing his likeness and honoring the former president at table eighteen, his favorite booth.

The structure was threatened in 1951 when a three-alarm fire swept through the second floor of the oyster house. Three firemen were injured, but the original raw bar and booths were unharmed. Some say the blaze stirred up spirits that had remained dormant for years.

In addition to its historical pedigree, which included kings, presidents and even actors like Matt Damon and Meryl Streep, the Union Oyster House has long-standing reservations for a few of the building's resident spirits. There are far-fetched accounts of President Kennedy's ghost making a return visit to his Sunday haunt. "The Kennedy family was known to be quite fond of the oyster house and JFK even has a booth dedicated to him," reported an online site, adding that patrons claimed to have spotted "Kennedy's apparition wandering near his booth."

Also, many believe that Daniel Webster, who notoriously devoured six plates of oysters while tossing back a tumbler of brandy almost daily, still holds court at the U-shaped oyster bar that bears his name. "Visitors to the Union Oyster House come not so much for the food as for the thrill of eating the same dish in the same spot as some of America's historical figures," mused an online restaurant site, alluding to former presidents like Calvin Coolidge, Franklin D. Roosevelt and Bill Clinton, who dined there when they visited Boston. "You can claim a stool at the raw bar and slurp oysters next to the ghost of Senator Daniel Webster, a regular who daily enjoyed his tumblers of brandy with oysters on the half shell." Webster became a

Union Oyster House, located at 41–43 Union Street, is so old that the original building, dating back to 1714 and erected a quarter of a century before Faneuil Hall, was waterfront property overlooking Boston Harbor. *Courtesy of the Boston Public Library, Print Department.*

Massachusetts senator in 1827, one year after the restaurant opened as the Atwood & Bacon Oyster House.

Bob Eshback, a veteran shucker and bartender at the Webster hangout, told me that he and other employees have experienced paranormal activity in the Union Oyster House's basement. Contrary to the ghostly rumors, the late nineteenth-century senator reportedly left the building years ago, and JFK hasn't made a postmortem comeback. When asked where Webster sat in the 1800s, Eshback said it was standing room only for the restaurant's most revered patron. "He didn't sit, he stood," Eshback responded. "There were no stools back then."

While Eshback claimed to be more of a skeptic than a believer, he said that he felt "a presence" or an odd energy emanating from the downstairs area when he started working for the restaurant in 1999. "There are reports of a busboy or a dishwasher committing suicide in the basement in the early twentieth century or possibly the late nineteenth century," Eshback explained. Eshback hasn't felt the ghostly energy in the past five years or so, but he avoided the storage area below when he first tended bar in the late '90s. "Many people who have worked here didn't like going down there because of the presence."

File under: phantom gourmet

Chapter 7

North End Haunts

Based purely on aesthetic, Boston's North End should be haunted. In fact, horror writer H.P. Lovecraft believed the neighborhood was fertile ground for the supernatural. In *Pickman's Model*, the author convincingly wrote about the inexplicable magic of the North End's spirited underbelly, adding that "the whole North End once had a set of tunnels that kept certain people in touch with each other's houses, and the burying ground and the sea." He also talked about the lack of ghosts in Boston's Back Bay, saying the newly created land around Newbury Street hadn't been around long enough "to pick up memories and attract local spirits."

Michael Baker, head of the group called the New England Center for the Advancement of Paranormal Science (NECAPS) and member of Para-Boston, leaves no gravestone unturned when he investigates a so-called haunted location, which includes a few of the old structures in the North End. Baker said he's heard very few reports of ghosts in the historic buildings surrounding Copp's Hill Cemetery. Why? He believes it's a cultural thing.

"The North End seems a bit devoid of claims," Baker said when asked about the lack of alleged paranormal activity in the historically Italian neighborhood. "I have always felt much of it has to do with the religious views of the people who live there. There are a lot of old-school Italian families there, people who tend to be well embedded in religious culture. I have noticed that this Old World approach to religion often brings with it an unspoken rule about dabbling in or acknowledging things related to the paranormal."

Old North Church, located at 193 Salem Street in Boston's North End, is where the "one if by land and two if by sea" signal was sent from the church's wooden steeple. *Courtesy of the Boston Public Library, Print Department.*

Baker's "real science, real answers" mantra cuts through the usual smoke and mirrors associated with the "Boo!" business. With Baker, there's no over-the-top *Ghostbusters* gear or fake Cockney accents. When it comes to science-based paranormal investigations, he's the real deal.

"Basically, there is no ghost-catching device," explained Baker. "The field has changed. It has taken more of a fun-house approach—it has become a novelty—and it has set the paranormal investigation field back in a way. A lot of people are trying to use a screwdriver to hammer a nail. People go in with preconceived notions, and if anything happens, they're going to come to a certain conclusion. If something moves [or] bumps or they hear footsteps, they're going to automatically assume that it's a ghost, and that's a bad way to investigate."

Baker continued: "Technology can't detect spirits...we have to prove that spirits exist before we can build anything that can measure them. There was a shift in the field, occurring in the '90s, where it's a game to mimic what is seen on television. There was a period where it was purely scientific, and now people think they can turn off the lights, pick up an infrared camera and capture a ghost."

Oddly, one of Boston's more infamous made-up ghost stories involves a man leaving his home from Middle Street in the North End. William Austin's Peter Rugg literary character—who stubbornly rode his horse into a thunderstorm in 1770 and was cursed to drive his carriage until the end of time—was completely fabricated. However, people over the years have reportedly spotted the ghostly man with his daughter by his side frantically trying to make the trek back to Boston.

According to the legend, Rugg was visiting Concord with his daughter and stopped by a tavern recommended to him by a longtime friend before

Michael Baker, head of the group called the New England Center for the Advancement of Paranormal Science (NECAPS), investigated several of the locations featured in *Haunted Boston Harbor*. He shows off his homemade electromagnetic spectrum sensor. No, it's not a prop from *Ghostbusters*. *Photo by Sam Baltrusis.*

heading back to Boston. A violent thunderstorm was heading in their direction and the watering hole's owner insisted that Rugg and his daughter stay the night. Rugg, a notoriously defiant old man, refused the offer and headed directly into the storm. The horse and its driver never returned to Boston. However, people claim to have seen what was called "the Stormbreeder," a phantom carriage driven by Rugg and considered to be the precursor to a thunderstorm, all over New England. One man in Connecticut said he had a face-to-face encounter with the ghost. "I have lost the road to Boston. My name is Peter Rugg," the specter supposedly said before vanishing into thin air.

For many, the only real ghosts that exist are the ones that haunt the insides of their heads.

"There are some claims in the North End," continued Baker. "I know there are stories about the tunnels there. I have had a few calls from the North End over the years, but unfortunately, they never amounted to anything significant."

Baker isn't ruling out the possibility of ghosts in the North End. However, he hasn't found anything substantial while investigating there and finds the locals to be unusually tight-lipped. "I know several old Italian families and they won't even embrace a discussion about ghosts," he said. "To them it's religiously forbidden. Of course, this is just my speculation but it's a pattern I've seen in people I speak with."

While the North End is mysteriously devoid of reported ghost sightings, the legends associated with its series of rumored underground tunnels seem to be based on reported fact. "There definitely were tunnels underneath the North End," explained Peter Muise, author of *Legends and Lore of the North Shore*. "For example, in the nineteenth century, construction workers discovered that a house at 453 Commercial Street had an archway in its cellar that connected to a large tunnel. It led from Commercial Street up toward Salem Street. Unfortunately, this house was demolished in 1906 and the tunnel entrance along with it."

Who built the tunnels? Muise said they were probably built in the 1700s by Thomas Gruchy, a privateer who became wealthy from raiding Spanish ships. "He invested his loot in several Boston businesses, including a distillery, a warehouse and several wharves. His wealth was excessive even for a privateer, and many of his neighbors suspected that he was somehow smuggling goods into Boston without having to pay the British tariffs. Despite his shady background he became a prominent member of Boston society. He purchased the Salem Street mansion of former Governor Phipps in 1745, threw lavish parties, and became a congregant at the Old North Church. Four plaster angels that he looted from a French ship still decorate the church today."

Gruchy mysteriously disappeared in the 1700s and left behind a legacy of underground tunnels and stolen goods. "At the height of his wealth and popularity Gruchy vanished from Boston and was never seen again," Muise explained. "It's believed that he was smuggling goods past the British using a series of underground tunnels, and fled town when they discovered what he was doing. Sadly his mansion on Salem Street was torn down years ago."

Muise said that many secrets are buried beneath the North End's bloodstained soil. "A few other North End tunnels have been found," he said. "A book from 1817 mentions a tunnel under a house on Lynn Street, and a guide to Boston architecture notes that the cellar of a house on Salem Street still has an entrance to a tunnel in its basement. It has been bricked off so it's not clear where the tunnel goes or what it was used for."

Perhaps the ghosts of the North End are hiding in these hidden tunnels? Yes, it's possible that they're lurking in the shadows beneath the cobblestone streets traveled by thousands of tourists flocking to a neighborhood famous for its old-school Italian eateries and Paul Revere.

Commercial Street

Based purely on the bizarre disaster that unfolded on January 15, 1919, the North End's Commercial Street is ground zero of one of Boston's more freakish *Twilight Zone*–style events. On an unusually warm January day, a large vat of molasses heated up and the sugary liquid used in the distillation of rum expanded beyond the capacity of its container. The tank, located at 529 Commercial Street, then burst.

A wave of 2.5 million gallons of molasses raced down the street. It was forty-feet high and moved at thirty-five miles per hour. The dark tide was so powerful that a truck was picked up and hurled into Boston Harbor. Twenty-one people were drowned or crushed in the not-so-sweet Great Molasses Flood, and at least one dozen horses were swallowed up by the deadly goo.

"Molasses, waist deep, covered the street and swirled and bubbled about the wreckage," reported the *Boston Post*. "Here and there struggled a form—whether it was animal or human being was impossible to tell. Only an upheaval, a thrashing about in the sticky mass, showed where any life was....Horses died like so many flies on sticky fly-paper. The more they struggled, the deeper in the mess they were ensnared. Human beings—men and women—suffered likewise."

More than 150 people suffered from injuries sustained during the disaster. Blocks were flooded. Cleanup crews used a fireboat to wash away the mess. The molasses swept into Boston Harbor and people tracked the sticky goo all

A wave of 2.5 million gallons of molasses raced down the street on January 15, 1919. Twenty-one people were drowned or crushed in the Great Molasses Flood. *Courtesy of the Boston Public Library, Print Department.*

over Boston—on the subway, in the streets and on their clothes. "Everything a Bostonian touched was sticky," reported *Smithsonian* magazine.

Ghost lore enthusiasts often ask if the Boston Molasses Flood has left a psychic imprint on Commercial Street. The dark tide may have caused what parapsychologists call an aura of disaster—fertile ground for the birthing of ghosts.

Visitors often report smelling molasses near 529 Commercial Street, even though the tragedy occurred almost one century ago. Sensitives to the paranormal often claim to feel a heaviness near the scene of the event.

Some ghostly activity has also been reported in the area, which may or may not be related.

In 1974, a sighting of a ghost ship near Commercial Wharf was reported. The crew of a local fishing vessel set sail one foggy night. After departing from the nearby Long Wharf, the boat passed near the site of the Great Molasses Flood. Suddenly, a residual haunting from Boston's past manifested in front of them.

"This was no ordinary ship," wrote Joseph Mont and Marcia Weaver in *Ghosts of Boston*. "Before the fishing vessel was a battered, barely seaworthy English frigate that appeared to be at least two centuries old. Not a man was seen on deck and not a soul was on the bridge."

As soon as the phantom frigate appeared, it vanished.

The fishing vessel was then engulfed in a mysterious fog. Soon after the visual encounter, the sailors picked up mysterious chatter on their radio. "Someone was trying to contact them," continued Mont and Weaver. "The message, however, consisted of what sounded like a group of men screaming obscenities in a Cockney accent. Whether it was anger or panic is unclear."

Based on old seafaring superstitions, it's bad luck to even mention a ghost ship sighting. One man on the small fishing boat did report the event to the Coast Guard. No rational explanation surfaced; it continued to be a Boston Harbor mystery.

Lewis Wharf, which is a stone's throw from the Great Molasses Disaster site, is home to a former boardinghouse for wayward ship captains and sailors who docked in Boston. Built in 1839, it was known as the Pilot House. Today, the structure's façade is a coffee shop and bank. Law offices and condos are also located in the building. Behind the structure is a green space, called Pilot House Park, which faces the water and connects to the 46.9-mile path known as the Boston Harborwalk.

According to multiple sources, the spirits of salty sea captains have been seen in the Pilot House. "People who have spent time in the building report hearing unintelligible voices of men permeating the halls," wrote Christopher Forest in *Boston's Haunted History*. "The clink and clatter of glass, with an occasional smash, also have been known to punctuate the night, heralding a rowdy day of old."

Forest said that a lady in white has been spotted throughout the Pilot House. She appears as a full-bodied apparition and is known to move objects and sometimes even closes doors. In addition to the woman in white, shadow figures have been spotted in the building. It's common for doors to open and close, as if spirits were trying to enter their rooms in the former overnight haunt.

"Even outside of the wharf, visitors and residents alike have claimed to see or feel something unnatural along the water," continued Forest. "Sometimes, this presence actually manifests itself in the form of an old sailor or captain wandering the wharf in search of a room at the Pilot House or maybe even a ship to board. Other times, the presence surfaces over the water, floating on the crest of waves appearing as orbs."

File under: dark water

OLD NORTH CHURCH

What really happened at Old North Church on April 18, 1775? The famous "one if by land, two if by sea" line from Henry Wadsworth Longfellow's poem "Paul Revere's Ride" is based on actual events orchestrated by Revere and carried out by Old North Church's sexton, or the church's caretaker, Robert Newman. Revere's friend and the church's vestryman, Captain John Pulling Jr., was also there to warn the Sons of Liberty that General Thomas Gage and his British troops were coming.

Two lanterns, held that fateful night at the top of Old North Church's wooden steeple, ignited what would become the beginning of the American Revolution.

Old North Church's former sexton had a close encounter with the misty outlines of three Revolutionary War–era men. *Photo by Sam Baltrusis.*

"Revere enlisted the help of over thirty additional riders. He placed them across the river in Charlestown and ordered the militia leaders to look to the steeple of Old North Church every night for signal lanterns, the number of which indicating when the British army was leaving Boston and by which route," the Old North Foundation explained on its website. "One lit lantern meant the British would march over the Boston Neck, a narrow strip of land and the only road connecting the town to the mainland, which would take a considerable amount of time. Two lit lanterns in the steeple meant the British would take a shortcut by rowing boats across the Charles River into Cambridge, cutting valuable time off their journey."

Newman climbed up the staircases in the back corners of Old North Church and scurried up eight flights of stairs in complete darkness. He lit two lanterns with flint and steel at the top of the steeple and held them for about one minute toward Charlestown, alerting Revere's men, who included the often overlooked William Dawes.

General Gage, who, coincidentally, worshipped at Old North Church, was greeted by an armed militia in Lexington. And the rest, as they say, is history.

With the church having played such an important role in the days leading up to the American Revolution, it should come as no surprise that it also brims with the spirits of those who lived and died there during its hundreds of years of tumultuous history. The late Jim McCabe, a noted ghost lore expert, believed the historic Revolutionary War–era buildings like Old North Church to be ghost magnets. "The old Yankees may have been strange in some ways, but they kept the old buildings, which has made it attractive to many visitors—even ghosts," McCabe told the *Boston Globe*. "Spirits are attracted to places they lived in. I think what attracts ghosts up here is that you don't tear down the buildings."

Built in 1723 by William Prince, Old North is the oldest standing church building in Boston. The famous steeple, which can be seen at various spots throughout Boston and the harbor, fell during Hurricane Carol in 1854. It was fully restored the following year. It was also blown down by the great gale in 1804 and rebuilt in 1807. And yes, Old North is believed to be haunted.

According to Pam Bennett, retail manager at the popular tourist attraction, the building's former sexton had a close encounter with the misty outlines of three Revolutionary War–era men. "He said they were as clear as day," Bennett told me, adding that the church's sexton was a skeptic and was a bit shocked to run into three full-bodied apparitions at the Salem Street church. "He told them that he [was] just doing his job, and he noticed their eyes followed him. When he returned, they were gone."

Bennett also mentioned that a woman who lived in the brownstone next to Old North banged on the gift shop door one day and claimed that a boy buried beneath the church regularly visited her North End home. "We told her that we do have unmarked graves beneath the church."

In fact, thirty-seven crypts, buried beneath the structure, contain the remains of over one thousand former members of Old North Church. But why would a nineteenth-century boy haunt the church's North End neighbor?

Salem Street Academy, a schoolhouse on the north side of the church property, was built in 1810. Boston's first Sunday school got its start at the academy, opening its doors to the city's children in 1815. Co-owned by the church, the Sunday school became popular and welcomed thousands of students, recalled Dr. Charles Downer in his account published in 1893. Henry Ward Beecher, a famous Civil War–era abolitionist, was one of the school's alumni. Beecher's sister, Harriet, penned the antislavery manifesto *Uncle Tom's Cabin*. The school was replaced by the parish house in 1848 and was officially closed in 1908.

Believe it or not, the woman who had a face-to-face encounter with the ghost boy wearing period garb lives in the exact location that was formerly home to Salem Street Academy. While no reports of untimely deaths at the school in the 1800s can be found, it's common for spirits to return to a place they frequented. "A person doesn't have to die at a location for it to become haunted," wrote Joni Mayhan in *Dark and Scary Things*. "They return because it's a comfortable place for them."

And what about the three Revolutionary War–era spirits spotted by Old North Church's sexton? Mayhan said it's common for ghosts to frequent churches because of guilt over a past deed. "If they feel their sin is great enough, they might balk at crossing over into the light out of fear of where it will bring them," Mayhan continued. "By dwelling at a church, they might feel closer to God and hope to find redemption for their sins."

Of course, hundreds of former parishioners are buried in the labyrinthine crypts in the bowels of Old North Church. While spirits find solace in these places of worship, the emotions associated with important events—like a marriage or even a funeral—can also linger within these hallowed and often historic walls.

File under: holy spirit

Stanza Dei Sigari

Nestled beneath the North End's Caffé Vittoria on Hanover Street is the cavernous Stanza dei Sigari, an old-school cigar parlor, which had a past life as a 1920s-era speakeasy. Established in 1929, Caffé Vittoria was the first Italian-style café in Boston. Meanwhile, the thriving hot spot's downstairs neighbor has a different claim to fame.

It's known as the North End's most haunted location.

Stanza dei Sigari made front-page news in March 2013, when the subterranean cigar parlor was featured on Syfy's *Haunted Collector*. According to the *Boston Herald*, manager David Riccio Jr. wasn't just blowing smoke when it came to reported paranormal phenomena.

He sent in a videotape to the show's producers stating that some of his customers and employees had been scared off by unexplainable activity experienced at his cigar bar.

"There's more than just smoke wafting through the air at Stanza dei Sigari," the *Herald* reported. "The North End cigar bar's workers are blaming

Stanza dei Sigari, an old-school cigar parlor on Hanover Street in Boston's North End, was featured in the Syfy Channel's *Haunted Collector*. *Photo by Sam Baltrusis.*

a paranormal presence for broken shelves, flashing lights and unexplained bumps in the night in the basement shop on Hanover Street."

Riccio said his family-owned business has a history of paranormal activity. "I've always, even when I was a kid, thought there were ghosts down there," he said.

The manager said employees witnessed plates flying off tables and lights turning on and off. A terrified waitress claimed that someone, or something, was standing behind her one night. When she turned around, she spotted a black shadow dart across the room and then escape through a glass door.

Brian J. Cano, an investigator with the now-defunct TV show *Haunted Collector*, wrote online that he was smitten with the location. "There is so much famous history in Boston and especially the North End, where our case was located. Honestly, I was surprised about the layout of this part of town," Cano wrote on his behind-the-scenes blog. "I found it to be very European, with thin, winding side streets barely wide enough for a single car, bistros, bakeries and bike riders everywhere. The chain stores and restaurants I was used to seeing were nowhere to be found and that was strangely comforting. Corny as it sounds, I really could feel the echoes of the past reverberating off of [*sic*] every brick in the road, every tree that swayed in the wind."

John Zaffis, the nephew of Ed and Lorraine Warren who specializes in removing any on-site trigger objects responsible for the location's reported paranormal activity, led the *Haunted Collector* investigation with Cano at Stanza dei Sigari. His team's findings were shocking.

The building was constructed in 1896, and the land had formerly been home to a "baby farm," a Victorian-era underground business, which, in exchange for cash, took children from parents who were unable to care for them and sometimes killed them.

The sixty-year-old Riccio was born in the building located at 292 Hanover Street and heard various tales from his father and grandfather about the structure's history, but he was shocked to learn about the sordid details involving children. "We were freaked out [that] it was a baby farm," he told the *Boston Herald*.

The baby farm was owned and operated by a woman named Miss Elwood who had a history of abusing babies left at the baby farm. According to research uncovered by the TV show, she might have killed a few of the orphaned infants using arsenic. Zaffis and his *Haunted Collector* crew found a medical kit containing an 1870s-era syringe hidden within the building's foundation.

Cano said the team spent days canvassing the location, ruling out other logical explanations for the paranormal phenomena, before team members stumbled on the nineteenth-century baby farm artifact. "At the café, we checked out the reports of cups and dishes flying off the shelves, the spinning wheel of the coffee grinder as well as the tommy gun encased above the back steps," Cano wrote. "There was so much to see and so much to check off the list there."

Once Zaffis removed the Victorian-era medical kit, the hauntings at Stanza dei Sigari reportedly stopped.

So what happened to the trigger objects confiscated by the *Haunted Collector* team? The crew's lead investigator, Zaffis, recently purchased the former McBride Funeral Home in nearby Adams, Massachusetts, and plans to showcase the haunted artifacts—including the syringe confiscated from Stanza dei Sigari—at his Museum of the Paranormal.

"Over the course of years I've collected quite a few items," the Connecticut-based Zaffis told the *Berkshire Eagle*. "They're out in my barn now, but I always thought it would be fun to have people see the items and hear the stories about how they are connected to hauntings."

Zaffis said the exhibit would operate on a rotating basis and would contain "a huge number of dolls from a number of cases, a haunted piano, haunted organ, statues, religious items, occult items, clothing, haunted books, a sewing machine, a haunted telephone, and a huge collection of haunted mirrors—they hold onto energy, they hold onto spirits."

File under: trigger object

Chapter 8

Pirate Haunts

Move over witches. The most vilified group among the colonial-era finger pointers was, in fact, the swashbuckling, "argh matey" set. Yep, pirates were arguably the most hated outsiders to ruffle the feathers of the notoriously intolerant settlers who fled to the new land seeking religious freedom.

Cindy Vallar, editor of the *Pirates and Privateers* newsletter, said early Bostonians demonized piracy more than the inhabitants of other cities, such as New York and Newport, Rhode Island, who treated their pirate visitors like rock stars. "The Puritan influence played a key role in Boston's history, and men like the Rev. Cotton Mather frequently preached on the evils of piracy. His sphere of influence was particularly strong and widespread," Vallar explained. "The colonial governors of Boston and Massachusetts were less tolerant of such crime."

Vallar, the Texas-based author of *Scottish Thistle*, told me that she noticed a clear negative bias toward the city's pirate interlopers. "Other places in the colonies didn't always see pirates in this same vein. They provided goods not available because of the Navigation Acts, and they provided a service—protection—in some places because England couldn't defend all of its possessions. Politics also played a role in whether they were demonized or treated like rock stars."

In fact, Boston's pirates were hanged and displayed in crude contraptions known as gibbet cages on Nix's Mate and Bird Islands in Boston Harbor. Vallar said the pirates were first hanged on what was then called Hudson's Point, which

Marked by a black-and-white stucco-covered day beacon mounted on a stone platform, Nix's Mate is a rocky shoal near the convergence of three major channels in Boston Harbor. *Photo by Frank C. Grace.*

is in the general vicinity of Commercial and Charter Streets in Boston's North End. "On the day of their hanging they were escorted by boat to Hudson's Point. That's where they were hanged on a gallows in the mud flats," Vallar said. "English tradition was that since the courts fell under admiralty law, the corpses had to be washed by three tides before they could be disposed of. John Quelch and his men were the first to be tried in Boston," she continued, adding that earlier pirates were transported to London because vice admiralty courts didn't exist before 1701.

Out of the handful of pirates tried in Boston, Vallar said three come to mind. "Captain William Kidd is probably the best known. Boston is where he was arrested on charges of murder and piracy. He was imprisoned here until he was transported to London to stand trial."

Vallar continued, "The second pirate is John Quelch. He's not well known, but he was the first pirate to be tried in an admiralty court outside England. The third pirate is William Fly, who refused to repent for his crimes—one of the few pirates not swayed by the Reverend Cotton Mather, or any minister, on the need to atone for his sins before dancing the 'hempen jig' or hanging."

In addition to the possibly true lore associated with William Fly on Nix's Mate, one legend is associated with an unmarked grave at the rear of King's Chapel Burying Ground on Tremont Street. People claim to hear the raucous laughter of a pirate echoing throughout the cemetery. Although the gravestone has no name, many believe it's the final resting place of the infamous pirate Captain Kidd.

According to Vallar, it's not. While the salty dog was definitely arrested in Boston in 1701 and was hanged and buried in England, little proof exists to either support or disprove the idea that he haunts the historic burying ground.

Why would local legend embrace this historically inaccurate ghost story? Vallar said revisionism is commonplace when it comes to pirates. "I think word of mouth plays a key role. It's kind of like the whisper down the lane. One person tells the story, but the next tweaks it, and the teller after that does the same until the original version and the revised version no longer resemble each other. It's what makes good storytelling."

Vallar said she hadn't encountered any good ghost stories while debunking misinformation associated with Boston's buccaneers. "My readers are more interested in the pirates while they were alive rather than after they died," she joked.

But there may be a kernel of truth associated with the King's Chapel legend. A lesser-known pirate was buried at King's Chapel Burying Ground. The body of John Lambert, a man executed for piracy, was confiscated and moved by his prominent Salem family and interred in an unmarked grave next to his deceased wife and son.

Perhaps Lambert is King's Chapel Burying Ground's pirate ghost? Shiver me timbers.

Lovells Island

Based on its proximity to Georges Island, it appears to be a stone's throw away from the backside of Fort Warren. However, looks can be deceiving. In fact, a strong undercurrent is reported in the waters, known as the Narrows, separating the two islands.

Lovells Island has seen many shipwrecks over the years. "Until a lighthouse was built, many a ship captain wrecked his vessel on the island," wrote W.C. Jameson in *Buried Treasures of the Atlantic Coast*. "This collision course has left a wealth of pirate's booty on the island's coast."

In December 1786, a small vessel carrying thirteen travelers from Damariscotta, Maine, was en route to Boston. Around midnight, the boat sank within swimming distance of Lovells Island. The passengers quickly

Lovells Island, which is believed to be named after William Lovell, who lived in Dorchester in 1630, is known for its buried treasure and "Lover's Rock," a nickname for the spot where a couple froze to death in an embrace. *Photo by Sam Baltrusis.*

found shelter on the island but the respite was short-lived. Eleven of the travelers froze to death overnight. Theodore Kingsbury, who was found in a wretched state of hypothermia the following morning, was transported to a hospital on the mainland but was pronounced dead upon arrival.

One couple, Sylvia Knapp and her unknown fiancé, was found the following morning beneath a rock. The two had frantically held each other to stay warm, but it hadn't been enough. Tragically, they were found locked together in a frozen embrace beneath "Lover's Rock," a nickname for the spot marking the couple's untimely death. "They were on the eve of being married," wrote M.F. Sweester in the *King's Handbook of Boston Harbor*, adding that the soon-to-be-wed lovers were heading to Boston to buy furniture for their new home in Maine.

A shipwreck occurred in 1767 involving a young girl, Susanna Haswell, who survived and later wrote about the childhood tragedy in the book *Rebecca*, also known as *The Fille de Chambre*. Haswell, renamed Rowson after marriage, wrote several tomes, including the bestselling book *Charlotte Temple*, which was published in 1791.

The island—which is believed to be named after William Lovell, who lived in Dorchester in 1630—is also known for its buried treasure. In 1782, a French warship known as the *Magnifique* hit the shoreline of Lovells Island and was abandoned. "There she lay for many years, a noble and melancholy wreck, until time and winter storms gradually broke her in pieces, or buried her under the sands of the sea," Sweester wrote.

Jameson said a huge stash of gold and silver coins went down with the sunken *Magnifique*. "The money formed the foundation of a French treasury to be established in America that would provide payment to soldiers for the procurement of needed supplies," he wrote. "Estimates of the kegs and chests of coins carried in the *Magnifique*'s hold has ranged from $350,000 to $4 million."

Several attempts were made to recover the lost treasures of the *Magnifique*, including a failed excavation in 1840. Edward Rowe Snow wrote in *The Islands of Boston Harbor*, "Again in July 1859, excavations were made, but all that the searchers could find were some beautiful pieces of wood from the hull of the ship."

In the early 1900s, Snow said keeper Charles H. Jennings was digging near the lighthouse on the island and surprisingly uncovered what looked like a gold coin. "He continued his excavations until he unearthed many of the round, flat disks," Snow reported. "Taking them into the house, he scrubbed and dug the deposit away from one of the objects, and there was revealed a gold coin."

Jennings vacated the island, leaving his assistant, Stewart Frasier, in charge. According to lore, Jennings returned to the spot where he uncovered the coin and found several deep holes. It's believed that Frasier uncovered the buried treasure and retired a wealthy man.

Speaking of buried treasure, a mysterious discovery came to light when the lighthouse was forced to relocate after the establishment of Fort Standish in 1900. "In 1902, the twin range lights were erected near Ram's Head, and when the foundation for the lower light was being dug the skeleton of a man was found far under the surface," wrote Snow. "Whether or not the bones guarded some pirate's treasure has not as yet been discovered. The remains had been petrified."

Regarding other legends associated with blundered pirate's booty, Lovells's quarantined neighbor, Gallops Island, is said to have been visited by Captain Kidd and Long Ben Avery. "During one trip, Avery is believed to have carried a fortune in diamonds to the island and buried it in a spot long since forgotten," wrote Christopher Forest in *Boston's Haunted History*. "Plenty of attempts to find the treasure have been made, most during the 1800s. Nothing was ever found."

Gallops Island, nicknamed "asbestos island," was closed in 2000 and has a past life as a restaurant, inn and quarantine station. It was home to three thousand Union soldiers during the Civil War and was occupied by a radio and cooking school during World War II. Asbestos was found in the military buildings, which have been closed until the carcinogen can be removed.

In addition to the legend of Avery's buried diamonds, pirate enthusiasts believe the infamous Captain Kidd made a pit stop on Gallops Island. "Some believe that his legendary treasure was buried on this island at some point in time," wrote Forest. "Like Avery's treasure, no proof has ever surfaced to support this idea."

Those who visited the island before its closure in 2000 remarked on the inexplicable supernatural energy that emanated from the drumlin's ruins. People who are sensitive to the paranormal have claimed that a strong, residual presence is associated with the quarantine hospital cemetery. Perhaps the ghosts of Gallops Island's past are trying to guide visitors to the location of the pirate's buried stash?

File under: treasure island

NIX'S MATE

Boston Harbor's smallest island is arguably its most mysterious. On Nix's Mate, reports have been made of a pirate specter known as William Fly, who was executed by hanging in the 1700s after apparently tying his own noose. Sailors who pass by the tiny, off-limits Nix's Mate claim to hear blood-curdling screams and maniacal laughter on the island, which was once used to showcase accused pirates such as Fly in a crude contraption known as a gibbet cage.

Cindy Vallar, editor of *Pirates and Privateers*, said Nix's Mate, along with the long-gone Bird Island, played a pivotal role in Boston's "argh matey" history. But the truth behind the eroded island's legend continues to be a mystery. "I don't know a lot about Nix's Mate," Vallar remarked. "Mostly I've come across it when researching pirate executions. The most famous pirate to hang here was William Fly. The island may have been named for a captain who was murdered by one of his men and later hanged here, or Nix may have been a pirate himself."

Marked by a black-and-white stucco-covered day beacon mounted on a stone platform, Nix's Mate is a dangerous rocky shoal near the convergence of three major channels in Boston Harbor. Its central location was crucial to the Puritans when they were looking to ward off potential pirates. "If a pirate was made an example of, his gibbeted corpse was placed where ships passing in and out of a harbor or estuary could see it," Vallar explained. "They served as warnings to all sailors that those who deigned to follow in the pirates' footsteps would meet a similar gruesome fate. Problem was that in the grand scheme of things most sailors who went on the account either died from other causes or were never caught and punished."

Peter Muise, author of *Legends and Lore of the North Shore*, said Nix's Mate was much larger four hundred years ago. "Records indicate the island had an area of twelve acres when it was deeded to one John Gallop in 1636 for sheep grazing. It currently has an area of about zero acres," Muise said.

What happened to all of the land, and how did the island get its bizarre name?

"According to legend, in the 1630s a first mate on a ship moored off the island was accused of murdering his captain while he slept," continued Muise. "The captain's last name was Nix. After a hasty trial the mate was found guilty and sentenced to be hanged on the island. Nix's mate protested that he was innocent, but his pleas fell on deaf ears."

The man allegedly cursed the island, begging God to prove he was accused of a crime he didn't commit. "Show that I am innocent," Nix's mate supposedly uttered. "Let this island sink into the sea to prove that I have never committed murder." Nix's mate was executed. Soon after, the island did start to sink into the harbor. However, erosion seems to be the cause—not some curse uttered by a soon-to-be-executed deckhand.

Muise said that a second, more fantastic variant of the Nix's Mate legend exists. It involves a role reversal. "Captain Nix was a pirate who got rich raiding merchant vessels," he recalled. "One night he rowed to the island with a chest full of gold and his loyal first mate. After the mate dug a pit, the captain killed him and buried him with the gold. His restless spirit guards the treasure but also apparently caused the island to sink into the sea."

Despite the legend's popularity, no reports exist of a man bearing his name. Nor are there any accounts of a pirate known as Captain Nix committing murder or being killed.

The third theory behind Nix's Mate's name involves the Dutch phrase "nixie shmalt," which refers to the haunting cry of water spirits. According to legend, a sailor from the Netherlands uttered the phrase while listening to the ghostly waves wallop the island's shore.

Muise said we'll probably never know for sure how Nix's Mate got its name. He also said the "sinking curse" is more based on legend than fact. "Historians claim it has shrunk over time simply because it was quarried for shale and ship's ballast in the 1700s," Muise explained. "After these large stones were removed, the tides eroded the rest of the island. That explanation makes sense, but somehow the stories about pirates and ghosts seem more fitting for this tiny but mysterious island."

Boston Harbor ferries and passengers who regularly sail by Nix's Mate en route to Georges Island in the outer harbor say a weird energy surrounds the tiny island. The *Provincetown III* got stuck in its rocky shoals on August 25, 2012, while heading from Boston to Provincetown. No injuries were reported, but it's common for captains to lose radio connection near Nix's Mate.

There are also more sinister reports. Locals believe that William Fly continues to linger on the rocky shoals as a harbinger of injustice. "On the island that is slowly succumbing to the ocean, sailors have reported seeing mysterious lights, hearing blood-curdling screams and uneasy laughs, as well as awkward whispers," claimed Christopher Forest in *Boston's Haunted History*. "Many speculate that the spirit of the violent pirate roams the island patrolling the land and calling to all sailors as they pass by."

Truthfully, Fly's ghost doesn't have much room to roam around Nix's Mate. It's almost completely submerged during high tide, except for a few rocks assembled in an odd pattern. Believe it or not, the configuration of the exposed rock looks like the perfect shape of a question mark, further punctuating Boston Harbor's freak of nature.

File under: pirate's curse

WHYDAH PIRATE MUSEUM

The Whydah Pirate Museum, located at 16 Macmillan Wharf on the tip of Cape Cod's Provincetown, boasts some priceless treasures believed to be cursed by a love-lost pirate keeping an eye on his stolen three-hundred-year-old booty.

The Whydah Pirate Museum in Provincetown is home to an allegedly enchanted pirate treasure. *Photo by Sam Baltrusis.*

The recovered gold from the pirate ship *Whydah* (pronounced "widdah"), which sank in a violent storm off Cape Cod in 1717, is rumored to be enchanted by "Black Sam" Bellamy. Apparently, the notorious pirate captain is still protecting his loot, which includes over ten thousand coins and four hundred pieces of Akan gold jewelry.

According to paranormal researchers who believe in the Stone Tape theory, inanimate objects like a pirate's treasure can absorb a form of energy from living people during intense moments in those people's lives.

"A residual haunting—trapped energy—is more likely stored by an item near the event," explained the authors of *Haunted Objects: Stories of Ghosts on Your Shelf*. "It becomes almost like a character…a crystal lamp or a setting of silverware becomes haunted and then replays the moment when the right tumblers fall into place. The object can be moved to another location and when the situation is right, the recording replays, creating a haunting."

The story behind Bellamy's enchanted treasure is rife with eighteenth-century drama.

"Sam Bellamy was in love. The object of his affection, according to Cape Cod lore, was Maria Hallett of Eastham, Massachusetts. Her parents liked Sam well enough but didn't think a poor sailor would make much of a husband. So in 1715 Bellamy went looking for his fortune," reported *National Geographic*. "He and his friend Palgrave Williams started out as ordinary treasure hunters, looking for shipwrecks. They found none. Rather than return empty-handed, the legend said, the determined lover became a pirate—"Black Sam" Bellamy. It was the perfect job for him. In just a year of raiding Bellamy and his crew plundered more than fifty ships on the Caribbean and Atlantic. They were getting rich—quick."

Based on the legend, the twenty-eight-year-old pirate with jet-black hair captured the three-masted ship *Whydah*. The vessel boasted twenty thousand pounds sterling of silver and gold earned from the lucrative sale of slaves, according to *National Geographic*. But the blood money was cursed: Bellamy's ship sank near the coast of Wellfleet on April 16, 1717. It's claimed that the pirate was holding on to his beloved gold as the stolen ship sank in a violent storm within a short distance of the Cape Cod shoreline.

While Bellamy was smitten with his booty, his love for Hallett was epic. Stories about his heartbroken girlfriend range from the absurd—like the fact that she was so resentful about his death that she sold her soul to the devil and became a witch—to the tragic. One story, told by Peter Muise in *New England Folklore*, suggested that "Maria remained faithful to Sam, watching and waiting patiently for his return. On the night of the storm she watched from the dunes, hoping the *Whydah* would make it safely to shore. When it didn't, she lost her mind from grief and ran down to the beach. The next day she was found on the shore, screaming and wailing as she wandered through the wreckage and drowned corpses."

Muise claimed that "her ghost is still said to walk near Marconi Beach in Wellfleet and her cries can be heard on dark stormy nights."

One twist on the story suggested that Hallett and Bellamy consummated their fiery romance and she gave birth to his child. "Maria was said to have given birth to a boy with black hair," wrote Mark Jasper in *Haunted Cape Cod*. "When she became pregnant she moved to a secluded spot in order to conceal her pregnancy, as townspeople of that era had no tolerance for unwed mothers." The child died in a freak accident by choking on straw, and Hallett was sent to prison for neglect. She escaped and was then called a witch.

Jasper also suggested that Hallett's ghost walks the dunes of Wellfleet. "Eyewitnesses have seen the ghostly apparition of a woman walking the cliffs and peering out at the sea for a lover who would never return," he wrote.

Apparently, Hallett's wailing specter has been spotted in various other locations throughout the Outer Cape. In 1998, a patron at a restaurant in Wellfleet claimed that the apparition of a young, blond female approached her in the restroom. Oddly, the woman who experienced this face-to-face encounter with Hallett's supposed ghost had a familiar last name: Bellamy.

"Black Sam" has not been able to rest in peace either. "Spirits associated with the *Whydah* continue to linger nearly three centuries later," wrote the Houston Museum of Natural Science. "Barry Clifford, discoverer of the *Whydah*'s remains, recounts in his book, *Expedition* Whydah, how the start of his 1998 exploration was plagued with constant, often inexplicable obstacles—engine problems, an undermanned crew, GPS malfunction, heavy fog, a shark encounter and more."

One crew member on Clifford's salvage vessel claimed that an eerie voice from beyond was heard over the radio speaker near the wreck site. The voice kept repeating: "We want your boat....We want your boat." Clifford's crewmen were so creeped out that they poured a bottle of rum overboard to make peace with the pirates. Apparently, it worked because the treasure hunters recovered the gold.

But the hauntings haven't stopped. The salty sentinel spirit at Whydah Pirate Museum in Provincetown is said to watch over the treasure. Bellamy called. He wants his booty back.

File under: paranormal pirate

BIBLIOGRAPHY

The material in this book is drawn from published sources, including issues of the *Boston Globe*, *Boston Herald*, *Boston Phoenix*, *Dig Boston*, *Patriot Ledger* and *Spare Change News*, and television programs like the Travel Channel's *Ghost Adventures* and Syfy's *Ghost Hunters* and *Haunted Collector*. Several books on Boston Harbor's paranormal history were used and cited throughout the text. Other New England–based websites and periodicals, like *Smithsonian*, *Yankee* and *National Geographic* magazines; LightHouseFriends.com; and Peter Muise's *New England Folklore*, served as sources. I also conducted firsthand interviews, and some of the material is drawn from my own research. My harbor-based ghost tour, Haunted Boston Harbor, was also a major source and generated original content. It should be noted that ghost stories are subjective, and I have made a concerted effort to stick to the historical facts, even if it resulted in debunking an alleged encounter with the paranormal.

Baltrusis, Sam. *Ghosts of Boston: Haunts of the Hub*. Charleston, SC: The History Press, 2012.

———. *Ghosts of Cambridge: Haunts of Harvard Square and Beyond*. Charleston, SC: The History Press, 2013.

———. *Ghosts of Salem: Haunts of the Witch City*. Charleston, SC: The History Press, 2014.

Bibliography

Balzano, Christopher. *Haunted Objects: Stories of Ghosts on Your Shelf.* Iola, WI: Krause Publications, 2012.

Bryson, Bill. *A Short History of Nearly Everything*. New York: Broadway Books, 2003.

D'Agostino, Thomas. *A Guide to Haunted New England.* Charleston, SC: The History Press, 2009.

Ford, Beverly, and Stephanie Schorow. *The Boston Mob Guide.* Charleston, SC: The History Press, 2011.

Forest, Christopher. *Boston's Haunted History*. Atglen, PA: Schiffer Publishing, 2008.

Hall, Thomas. *Shipwrecks of Massachusetts Bay*. Charleston, SC: The History Press, 2012.

Hauk, Dennis William. *Haunted Places: The National Directory.* New York: Penguin Group, 1996.

Jameson, W.C. *Buried Treasures of the Atlantic Coast.* Little Rock, AR: August House, 2006.

Jasper, Mark. *Haunted Cape Cod & the Islands.* Yarmouthport, MA: On Cape Publications, 2002.

Mayhan, Joni. *Dark and Scary Things*. Gardner, MA: Joni Mayhan, 2015.

Mont, Joseph, and Marcia Weaver. *Ghosts of Boston.* Boston: Snakehead Press, 2002.

Nadler, Holly Mascott. *Ghosts of Boston Town: Three Centuries of True Hauntings.* Camden, ME: Down East Books, 2002.

Revai, Cheri. *Haunted Massachusetts: Ghosts and Strange Phenomena of the Bay State.* Mechanicsburg, PA: Stackpole Books, 2005.

Snow, Edward Rowe. *The Islands of Boston Harbor*. Carlile, MA: Commonwealth Editions, 2008.

Sweester, M.F. *King's Handbook of Boston Harbor*. Boston: Houghton, Mifflin & Co., 1888.

Trettenero, MaryLee. *We're Still Here: The Secret World of Bunker Hill's Historical Spirits*. Boston: Happy Otter Press, 2015.

Weeks, Kevin, and Phyllis Kara. *Brutal: My Life Inside Whitey Bulger's Irish Mob*. New York: HarperCollins, 2006.

Zwicker, Roxie J. *Haunted Pubs of New England: Raising Spirits of the Past.* Charleston, SC: The History Press, 2007.

About the Author

Sam Baltrusis, author of *Ghosts of Boston*, *Ghosts of Salem* and *13 Most Haunted in Massachusetts*, is the former editor in chief of several regional publications, including *Spare Change News*, *Scout Somerville* and *Scout Cambridge*. He has been featured as Boston's paranormal expert on the Biography

Author Sam Baltrusis stands in front of the Wigwam Western Summit in North Adams after taping a segment for the TV show *13 Most Haunted in Massachusetts*. *Photo by Frank C. Grace.*

Channel's *Haunted Encounters*. As a side gig, Baltrusis moonlights as a guide. He has launched the successful ghost tours Boston Haunts and Cambridge Haunts and spearheaded a boat tour in 2014 called Haunted Boston Harbor. Baltrusis is also a sought-after lecturer who speaks at dozens of paranormal-related events scattered throughout New England, including an author discussion at the Massachusetts State House. In the past, he has worked for VH1, MTV.com, *Newsweek* and ABC Radio and as a regional stringer for the *New York Times*. Visit HauntedBostonHarbor.com for more information.

Visit us at
www.historypress.net

This title is also available as an e-book

www.ingramcontent.com/pod-product-compliance
Lightning Source LLC
Chambersburg PA
CBHW060806100426
42813CB00004B/968
* 9 7 8 1 5 3 1 6 9 9 2 6 0 *